The Last Voyage of the Karluk

The Last Voyage of the Karluk

A Survivor's Memoir of Arctic Disaster

William Laird McKinlay

St. Martin's Griffin

New York

Library of Congress Cataloging-in-Publication Data

McKinlay, William Laird.
    The last voyage of the Karluk : a survivor's memoir of Arctic
    disaster / William Laird McKinlay ; foreword by Magnus Magnusson.
        p. cm.
    Originally published: Karluk. London : Weidenfeld and Nicolson,
© 1976.
    Includes index.
    ISBN 0-312-20655-0
    1. Karluk (Ship). 2. Arctic regions—Discovery and exploration.
3. Canadian Arctic Expedition (1913–1918).   I. McKinlay, William
Laird.   Karluk.   II. Title.
G370.K37M315   1999
919.804—dc21
                                                        99-17672
                                                            CIP

First published in the United States under the title *Karluk: The Great Untold Story of Arctic Exploration* by St. Martin's Press

First St. Martin's Griffin Edition: June 1999

10 9 8 7 6 5 4 3 2 1

Contents

Foreword

The first man to reach the North Pole, Admiral Robert Edwin Peary (in 1909), made his last public appearance at a ceremony in Washington DC a few months before his death in 1920. Defying doctors' orders, he attended the presentation of the Hubbard Medal, the highest honour of the National Geographic Society of America, to a Canadian explorer, Vilhjalmur Stefansson. Stefansson, born of Icelandic parents, was being honoured for his leadership of the Canadian Arctic Expedition of 1913–1918, the last great Arctic expedition unsupported by wireless or aeroplane, and Peary spoke in glowing terms of how Stefansson had 'added more than 100,000 square miles to the maps ... outlined three islands entirely unknown before ... [outlined] the delineation of the continental shelf, filling-in ... unknown gaps in the Arctic archipelago....'

Stefansson, he said, was 'the last of the old school' of Arctic explorer, 'the worker with the dog and the sledge, among whom he easily holds a place in the first rank'. Another famous American explorer, General Adolphous Washington Greely, described Stefansson's five and a half years with the Canadian expedition as 'the world's record for continuous Polar service', and handed over the coveted Hubbard Medal 'in recognition both of the idealistic spirit and of the geographic importance of the discoveries made by Vilhjalmur Stefansson'. The distinguished company thundered their applause, and there is no doubt that this rather likeable man, an anthropologist and a writer of no mean ability, was deserving of praise for his studies of Eskimo life and his pioneer work in what General Greely called 'living on the game of the region, whether on the ice-covered sea or on the northern lands'. Nor was there any quarrel when the General, following the fashion of crediting the leader of an expedition with the achievements of his whole team, declared that: 'Besides the natural history and geologic knowledge . . . his hydrographic work is specially important, in surveys and in magnetic declinations. His numerous soundings not only outline the continental shelf from Alaska to Prince Patrick Island, but also disclose the submarine mountains and valleys of the bed of Beaufort Sea.'

But there was an omission on that night of celebration and eulogy, an omission that saddened many hearts and angered not a few: there was no mention of the *Karluk*. The *Karluk* was the leading ship of Stefansson's 1913–18 Arctic Expedition, and it was lost almost before the expedition had properly begun. Trapped in the Arctic ice, it drifted away on an ice floe while Stefansson was off on a caribou hunt; and while the leader continued with his explorations in the north, not returning for five years, the *Karluk* drifted for months in the ice pack before being crushed and sinking. Her entire complement of twenty-five, made up of crew, scientists and Eskimos (including a woman and two children) escaped on to the ice, thanks to the leadership of the ship's commander, Captain Robert Bartlett, who thereupon set off, with one Eskimo and dog-sled, on a hazardous 700-mile journey across the ice to Siberia for help. He reached his destination safely, but it was six months before rescue finally arrived, and by that time eleven men were dead. Eight died trying to reach the land across the heaving ice floes. One man shot himself. Two died of malnutrition and disease on ice-covered Wrangel Island, where the rest barely managed to survive until rescue came.

Stefansson was able to give only a second-hand report of the fate of the *Karluk* and her survivors as an appendix to his account of the expedition, *The Friendly Arctic*, published in 1921 by the MacMillan Company of Canada. In his book, *The Last Voyage of the Karluk*, Captain Bartlett told his story of the helpless drift in the pack ice through the continuous night of an Arctic winter, the landing on Wrangel Island and his own dash for help to Siberia.

But no one on the *Karluk* who escaped on to the ice and survived the awful privations of Wrangel Island has told the whole story of what happened during that first tragic year of the Stefansson expedition . . . until now.

William Laird McKinlay, a young Glasgow schoolteacher, was magnetician and meteorologist on the expedition. He escaped from the *Karluk*, lived through the nightmare of Wrangel Island, and is today a sprightly 88-year-old living in retirement in Glasgow. For sixty years he has kept silent about what happened on the expedition, partly because his memories were so painful, and partly because he had no wish to join in the recriminations, accusations and apportioning of blame contained in Stefansson's books (*The Friendly Arctic* and *The Adventure of Wrangel Island*) and in newspaper and magazine articles that followed their publication.

But McKinlay could never forget the *Karluk*, nor his dead companions. The memory haunted him throughout his service as an officer on the Western Front in the 1914–18 war, his years as a headmaster in Greenock, his otherwise happy retirement in Glasgow. He felt that the reputations of his colleagues had been tarnished by inaccurate reports and even deliberate distortions. He also resented criticism of the conduct of Captain Bartlett, whom he considered to be the only surviving hero of the entire affair, and who was honoured by the Royal Geographical Society of London for his rescue operation, as well as receiving the Hubbard Medal for his long service in the Arctic. McKinlay became consumed by a determination to set the record straight on what he calls 'the whole Stefansson myth'. While giving the man full credit for his studies of Eskimo life, his trail-blazing journeys across the Arctic floes, his undoubted skill at hunting and orientating himself in the Arctic, his literary style that won over scholar, scientist and layman alike, and his knack for public relations that salvaged a kind of glory out of the most impossible disasters, McKinlay believes that Stefansson was the wrong man to lead an expedition of such scale and importance, and so fraught with danger. He believes that the Stefansson expedition was ill-conceived, carelessly planned, badly organized, haphazardly manned and almost totally lacking in leadership. Because of this, men died needlessly and those who survived were put to tests of endurance and character that were unnecessarily severe. The main factor of blame was Stefansson's theory on which the whole enterprise was based – that the Arctic was a friendly place, where a man with a gun, a sledge and a dog team could survive indefinitely 'off the land', even when the 'land' was miles of drifting ice floes.

This was no doubt true of Stefansson himself, with his own hunting skill (in one book he describes how to wipe out an entire herd of caribou single-handed) and a couple of chosen companions working as a team under his personal tutelage. But Stefansson had a preference for recruiting what he called 'young men trained in the sciences and recently graduated from college' to do his scientific work, young men who had never been farther from home than the nearest university, who cheerfully set out for Stefansson's 'friendly Arctic' armed only with a degree, a thirst for adventure, good health, boundless enthusiasm and implicit faith in their leader.

When William McKinlay was marooned on the Arctic ice he was only twenty-five years old, and the only Polar bears he had ever seen were at Edinburgh Zoo. He had never handled a gun. Few of his companions knew anything about hunting, apart from the Eskimos in the party and one 'soldier of fortune', as McKinlay calls him, who had been knocking around the Arctic almost all his life and, like Stefansson, had spent years living among Eskimos. The First Officer on the *Karluk*, Sandy Anderson, who was one of the first to die, was only twenty years old.

There was no programme of Arctic training for the uninitiated, no acclimatization, no practice in the skills of survival – how to track a seal, kill a bear, skin a walrus, construct a kayak, build an igloo or put up a tent in a snowstorm; how to make a pair of sealskin trousers, gauge wind direction from the marks on a snowdrift, judge the safety of ice to bear a heavy sledge; how to keep warm, keep dry; how to sustain oneself with no instructions on diet, the importance of fresh meat, the dangers of too much protein, the best ways of cooking. There were experts in many fields on the expedition, but the party was split up almost from the word go, and at the first moment of crisis – the breaking-away of the *Karluk* from its land-locked anchorage on the ice pack – inexperienced scientists and crew members were deprived of their leader and all the knowledge and expertise of survival on which the whole enterprise was based.

The expedition's doctor, Scots surgeon Alistair Mackay, a veteran of Shackleton's Antarctic expedition of 1909 (when they got within ninety-seven miles of the South Pole) was one of the first to die on the ice, along with forty-six-year-old James Murray, another Scot who had been with Shackleton. Even men of such experience as Mackay and Murray, who had crossed the land ice around the South Pole, were ill-prepared for the treacherous conditions of the North Polar ice cap, which covers an ocean. Exposing inexperienced men to such conditions was almost like sending a bunch of untrained scientists to fend for themselves on the moon. Captain Bartlett had skippered Peary's *Roosevelt* in the successful expedition to the North Pole, and was an experienced navigator in Arctic waters, but he had not Stefansson's faith in the friendliness of the Arctic, and after the sinking of the *Karluk* he set out at once to bring help before it was too late. He was accustomed to commanding a ship, choosing a crew and seeing that they pulled together as amicably as possible, and he knew well that dangers other than starvation and death from exposure faced a crowd of ill-assorted men, forced to live together for months, perhaps years, under conditions of the utmost physical and psychological strain, three-quarters of the time in almost total darkness, completely cut off from the outside world, and leaderless. The situation called for not only technical skills which none of them possessed, but a high degree of moral fibre, mental stability, team spirit and comradeship. No attempt had been made to hand-pick the members of the expedition with these qualities in mind. They were a motley collection of scientists and sailors, with the usual crop of human frailties. One man was even a drug addict! To McKinlay's mind the worst feature of the months on Wrangel Island was the absence of real comradeship and the team-spirit that good leadership inspires. On Wrangel Island the men did just that – wrangle; they wrangled over food, over duties, over sharing ammunition. There was lying, cheating, stealing, malingering, as well as a lot of courage and humanity, particularly in the devoted care shown to the sick.

McKinlay has come to realize the terrible amateurism of the Stefansson expedition with increasing horror in the light of modern expertise and organization in the business of exploration. It was the heyday of the amateur, the time when men tried to climb Everest in knickerbockers and Norfolk jackets, when Britain was going wild with pride over Scott's brave but tragic failure to be first to reach the South Pole – another exercise in splendid amateurism. The Norwegian explorer, Roald Amundsen, who got there a month before Scott, had displayed a new professionalism in his attitude to the business of exploration. His expedition was better planned, prepared, equipped and controlled than the slap-happy world

of exploration had ever imagined. His opinion of Stefansson's casual attitude to the dangers of the Arctic was given in his autobiography, *My Life
as an Explorer* (1927): 'Some adventurous spirits seeking a fresh thrill in
the North may be misled by this talk about the "friendliness" of the Arctic,
and will actually attempt to take advantage of this "friendliness", and
adventure into these regions, equipped only with a gun and some
ammunition. If they do, certain death awaits them.'

Yet despite the eleven deaths on his 1913–18 expedition, Stefansson
never lost faith in his 'friendly Arctic', and in 1920 he sent a private expedition of four men and an Eskimo girl to 'colonize' the ill-fated Wrangel
Island, with provisions for six months to last them a possible two years.
Only the Eskimo girl survived. In *The Adventure of Wrangel Island*, Stefansson claimed that if the four young men (two of them aged nineteen and
twenty) had followed his instructions they would have survived, and re-
affirmed his conviction that white men could live in polar regions 'into
which Eskimos were unwilling to go because they believed them devoid
of resources'.

As the news of yet another tragedy on Wrangel Island reached William
McKinlay he began to compile a dossier on Stefansson's Arctic ventures.
He read every scrap of evidence he could lay his hands on, corresponded
with the survivors and the relatives of the dead men. He acquired copies
of the diaries of the victims to add to his own carefully kept log, along
with all the official reports and correspondence from the Canadian
National Archives. For more than half a century he has studied and ana-
lyzed, checked and cross-checked every word published by Stefansson,
Bartlett and the great explorers of the day. Captain Bartlett died in 1946.
Vilhjalmur Stefansson died in 1962. William McKinlay is the only known
survivor of any of the Stefansson expeditions. McKinlay's dossier is complete and his verdict on Stefansson, the explorer, is ready to be passed
to the Canadian Archives. But first he has been persuaded to tell the
story of the *Karluk* and Wrangel Island as he saw it. He says: 'I do
not wish to detract in any way from the achievements of Vilhjalmur
Stefansson, but the record must be put straight. I owe that to the
memory of my dead comrades, and to Captain Robert Bartlett, who
saved my life.'

This is his story, plain and unvarnished. It is a notable addition to the annals of Arctic exploration, a story of real heroism under appalling conditions, a noble epitaph for men who gave their lives to the quest for knowledge. Even if that quest was ill-conceived, it does not diminish their courage, nor their contribution to the story of mankind.

Magnus Magnusson

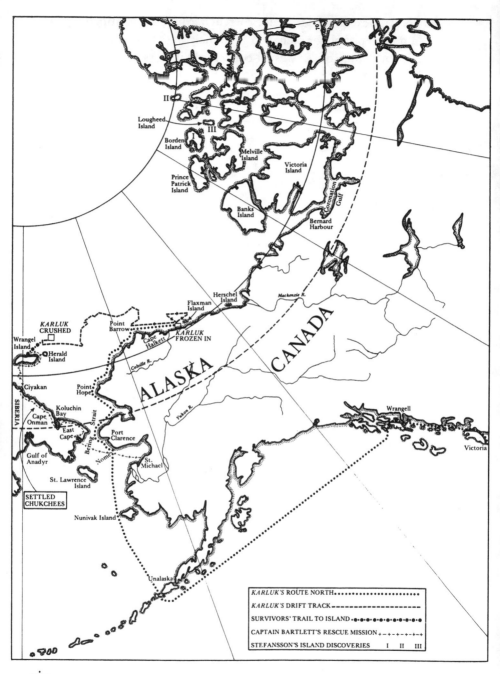

The Telegram

The telegram arrived at ten-past seven. It was Wednesday, 23 April 1913, and I had finished my evening meal and was settling down with my pipe and the evening paper when the doorbell rang. That telegram remained one of my mother's most treasured possessions until Hitler's bombers destroyed her home in Clydebank. I cannot remember its exact wording, but I still recall vividly the thrill I felt when I read it. Was I willing to join an Arctic expedition for four years? No salary, but all expenses paid. It was signed 'Stefansson'.

I was flabbergasted. Me! William Laird McKinlay, aged twenty-four, teacher of mathematics and science in Shawlands Academy, Glasgow, invited to be an explorer in the frozen wastes of the Arctic Circle! Me! Only five feet four, 'Wee Mac' to my friends (and to the boys at school behind my back) being asked to join the ranks of boyhood heroes like Nansen, Peary, Amundsen, Captain Scott! Reports were still coming in of the deaths of Scott's party on their way back from the South Pole after being beaten to the post by Amundsen.

The telegram might have been somebody's idea of a joke, like some present-day schoolboy sending his teacher a fake invitation to join the latest expedition to the moon, except that Arctic expeditions were almost a kind of international sport at the end of the nineteenth and the beginning of the twentieth century; and since there seemed to be very little in the way of land left to be discovered, scientists were in great demand to bring back technical information about the nature of things above and below the vast ice caps surrounding the Poles. As a Bachelor of Science and winner of a Scholarship in Mathematics and Natural Philosophy at Glasgow University, I had got to know Dr W.S. Bruce, the Scottish explorer, and for two years I had been helping him to collate observations made in the Scottish Antarctic Expedition of 1902–4. Dr Bruce knew my qualifications to do magnetic and meteorological work, and he knew I would jump at the chance of joining an exploration team

I rushed to a telephone and contacted Dr Bruce at home in Edinburgh, only to be told that he was in London, helping a Mr Stefansson select oceanographical equipment and scientific staff for an Arctic expedition. 'Stefansson' was the signature on my telegram, and as I waited to be put through to Dr Bruce's London hotel, I vaguely recalled newspaper stories about a Canadian anthropologist called Stefansson who claimed to have found a race of 'Blond Eskimos' during exploration of the Arctic coast of north-west Canada. Dr Bruce confirmed that on his recommendation, this was the man who was inviting me to join his latest expedition.

Vilhjalmur Stefansson was planning to explore far into the frozen north, between the northernmost shores of Canada and the North Pole. It was to be a vast scientific project, financed by the Canadian Government, involving anthropological study of the Eskimos, geological surveys (with a particular view to finding copper), sounding of uncharted Arctic waters, as well as a look-out for new islands to be discovered for Britain. I would be magnetician and meteorologist in the team if I wanted to go.

'Yes!' I shouted down the line.

Could I leave at once to make final arrangements in London?

Yes, again.

An hour later I was on the night train to London. It is only now that I fully realize the shock all this must have been to my mother: to have me snatched from home at a moment's notice, her William, who was so small and weakly at birth that the doctor gave him a year to live; Wee Mac, suddenly whisked away to be an explorer in the frozen Arctic! Dr Bruce had said I should be prepared to be away from three to four years. Nobody mentioned the very real possibility that I would never come back at all. And I have no recollection of any protest from my parents, any raising of doubts, or any sign of dismay. My mother just packed my overnight bag and promised to explain my absence to the headmaster of the school. I would be back on Friday morning to straighten things out with the School Board and collect the rest of my luggage before sailing from Glasgow on Saturday.

I slept very little on the journey to London. Sitting upright in a third-class compartment as the *Royal Scot* rushed southwards, I went over and over in my mind everything I remembered having heard or read about Arctic exploration, trying to visualize the adventures that lay ahead, shoving to the back of my mind, with youthful abandon, the reports of death and disaster that were so much a part of Arctic history. Exploration of the vast north and south polar regions was on the threshold of being revolutionized by the use of the wireless and the aeroplane. Soon, any expedition snowed-in or trapped in the Arctic ice, and short of supplies, would be able to radio its position and have supplies dropped from the air, or have rescue speeded-up by air search and airlift. But in 1913 Arctic exploration was an extremely hazardous business, little advanced in technique since Leif Eriksson had sailed his Viking ship westwards from Greenland to the shores of North America a thousand years before. Only the steam turbine had been added to help ships through the Arctic pack-ice, and when the ice really closed in, a ship with an engine was every bit as helpless as any of the sailing vessels that had been trapped, crushed and sunk without trace in attempts to circumnavigate the globe at its northernmost tip.

Boys like me had been bred on stories of the search for the North-West and North-East Passages, those elusive sea routes by which men sought to shorten the distance from Europe to China by going round the narrow top of the world, either eastwards or westwards, instead of zig-zagging southwards across the globe and going round it at a much larger point of circumference: westwards via Cape Horn, or eastwards via the Cape of Good Hope. We boys knew that Nordensjold had been first to follow the north-east route successfully, from 1878–9, sailing from the Atlantic eastwards round the north coast of Siberia, through the Bering Sea and the Bering Strait into the Pacific. On the big shiny map that hung over the blackboard at Clydebank School, we had followed Amundsen's slow progress in the first complete sailing of the North-West Passage, from 1903–5, taking the left-hand turn, as we thought of it, round the north coast of Canada, through the Beaufort Sea, then via Bering Strait to the Pacific Ocean.

How well we knew the names of all those others who had braved that forbidding wilderness of ice-packed ocean encircling the North Pole:

3

George Washington De Long, the American explorer, who had tried to reach the Pole via the Bering Strait in 1879, but had to abandon his ship, the *Jeannette*, in the pack-ice, and died with twenty of his crew, trying to reach the Siberian coast: Fridjof Nansen the Norwegian who in 1893 deliberately let his ship, the *Fram*, get frozen in the ice north of Siberia and drift north to a latitude of 84° N. from which point he and a companion left the ship and travelled across the ice by sledge to the highest latitude then attained, 86° 14′ N.; the specially built *Fram* escaped from the ice unscathed. As students in Glasgow we had thrilled to the news in 1909 that America's Admiral Peary had reached the North Pole, the first man to do so, at his eighth attempt. He got there just ahead of Amundsen, who then turned his attention to the Antarctic and made a dash for the South Pole, beating Scott there by a month, in 1911.

But it was the North Polar region and the vast unexplored area north of the Beaufort Sea that I would be sailing for in less than three days' time. This great white wilderness, which Peary had crossed to its ultimate point of latitude, 90° N. – the North Pole – was generally accepted to be composed of ice-covered Polar sea, but so few explorers had ever penetrated the 'Zone of Comparative Inaccessibility' (Peary just made a quick dash across the shortest line of approach, from the tip of Ellesmere Island, near Greenland) that there was no real proof as to whether it was in fact all sea or whether the ice might be concealing a mass of land. Vilhjalmur Stefansson was one of those who believed that there might well be undiscovered land north of the Beaufort Sea, and he had persuaded the Canadian Government to finance this expedition to explore the uncharted regions between the north of Canada and the North Pole.

I learned all this, and much more about Stefansson's plans, from the newspapers when I arrived in London. Stefansson had already left for Canada, but he had been interviewed before he left, and I read that I was going to be part of a team whose leader had hopes of discovering a new continent! As he wrote later in a dispatch to the Canadian *Victoria Times* (June, 1913):

The sensational aspect of the Canadian Arctic Expedition is that if it should prove as successful as it conceivably may be, then it will close forever the chapter of geographical discovery, for the only place on the whole earth where there can possibly be land of conceivable extent whose very existence is unknown to us, is the unexplored area of a million or so square miles that is represented by white patches on our map, lying between Alaska and the North Pole. Whether or not we found land, Stefansson had assured the Canadian Government that we would bring back information that would transform the maps of the world.

There would be a scientific staff of fifteen, headed by Stefansson as anthropologist, with Dr Rudolph Anderson, a Canadian zoologist, as second-in-command; another anthropologist, Diamond Jenness; two topographers, Kenneth Chipman and John Cox; a botanist and marine biologist, Fritz Johanssen; geologist John O'Neill (a copper expert); photographer George Wilkins (later Sir Hubert Wilkins, who made a pioneer flight in 1928 from Alaska to Spitzbergen, and in 1931 failed in an attempt to reach the North Pole by submarine – a prophetic dream of Stefansson's not realized until 1958 by the American atomic submarine *Nautilus* (which entered beneath the Arctic ice-cap, off Point Barrow, Alaska, and emerged in the Greenland Sea). There was another geologist, George Malloch; an assistant topographer, Bjarne Mamen; another anthropologist, Henri Beuchat; a secretary, Burt McConnell; and three Scots: Alistair Forbes Mackay, surgeon; James Murray, oceanographer; and myself, magnetician and meteorologist.

According to Stefansson this team, 'a larger staff of scientific specialists than have ever been carried on a Polar expedition', would investigate tides, currents, the depth and character of the Arctic sea bed, the temperature, chemical composition, and vegetable and animal life of the North Pacific and Arctic Oceans.

I was given more information when I met the Canadian High Commissioner at eleven o'clock that Thursday morning in London. I was formally signed on as a member of the expedition, and at noon the High Commissioner lifted the telephone and booked a passage for me on the Allen liner, *Grampian*, due to sail from Glasgow at noon on Saturday. I learned that the Canadian Government was sparing no expense. The very latest in scientific equipment had been bought on the advice of Dr Bruce, and when I got to Canada I was to have a three-weeks' course to acquaint me with the instruments I would be using. Dr Bruce and the Canadian officials I met answered as many of my questions as they could, and from what they told me, and from more newspaper cuttings, I was beginning to form a picture, as I steamed back to Glasgow on the night train, of the man to whom I was entrusting my life for the next three or four years.

Vilhjalmur Stefansson was thirty-four, the son of Icelandic parents who had emigrated to Canada. He was an anthropologist by profession, and the main reason for his explorations in the Arctic up till now had been to learn everything he could about the Eskimos. He had already made two expeditions (1906–7 and 1908–12) from which he had returned with a report of a 'new race of men', the so-called 'Blond Eskimos', and with more than fifty-thousand specimens, including species of caribou (reindeer) hitherto unknown, and more skulls of Barren Ground grizzlies than were in the possession of the scientific museums of the world. He also came back with a firm conviction that the unexplored regions around the North Pole, into which even the Eskimos refused to travel, were not the white wilderness that men imagined, but probably rich in minerals, such as copper, and that it was possible for men to live off the wild life of the Arctic by using the hunting skills of the Eskimo. This was the basis of Stefansson's great theory of the 'friendly Arctic', and perhaps it was just as well for my peace of mind that I was unaware of the great Amundsen's opinion that if men tried to take advantage of this 'friendliness' and adventured into the Arctic regions equipped only with a gun and some ammunition, 'certain death awaits them'.

I was well on my way to the Arctic before our leader started sending dispatches which declared that:

... the attainment of the purposes of the expedition is more important than the bringing-back safe of the ship in which it sails. This means that while every reasonable precaution will be taken to safeguard the lives of the party, it is realised both by the backers of the expedition and the members of it, that even the lives of the party are secondary to the accomplishment of the work! ... that the expedition is thoroughly equipped is all that we can say of it at present. The character of its management will develop from day to day, and it will only be some years from now, if no disaster overtakes us, that it will be possible to decide the relative value of the factors that make for its success for failure.

Looking back I can see in statements like these foreboding of the disasters to come, but that night as I was setting out on my great adventure, there was nothing to shake my confidence in the ability of this great man, Stefansson, to take our expedition to the Arctic and bring us all safely home again. All I read were eulogies of him, such as the one from his great friend, the conqueror of the North Pole, Admiral Peary: 'In personality and from training and experience, Stefansson is especially fitted for this work; his courage and control of untoward circumstances have been proved in the six years he has already put in on Arctic investigations, and he has shown executive ability and judgement in his plans for organisation of the new expedition.'

I learned that our leader was 'a man of middle height, strong of frame, with no superfluous flesh ... he tells you frankly he makes no pretensions as an athlete. He never walks where it is possible to ride, takes little or no exercise of any description. Yet his powers of endurance seem phenomenal, and far in excess of those of the trained athlete in hard condition.' With all this added to his training as an anthropologist and his 'qualities of a dreamer', Admiral Peary felt that he must congratulate the scientific world and the Canadian Government that Stefansson 'has stepped forth to do a man's work in Arctic exploration'.

With such stirring sentiments ringing in my head, I stepped off the train in Glasgow on Friday morning, with thirty-six hours left to sailing time.

First I had to straighten things out with my School Board, with whom I had a contract requiring a month's notice. Fortunately the members of the Board were meeting that morning in the Rector's room, and before the meeting began I was called in. Everyone had read about my appointment in the morning papers and I was showered with congratulations and good wishes before being granted formal and immediate leave of absence. I dashed to Queen Street station to catch the train to Edinburgh where I met Dr Bruce, back by now at the Scottish Oceanographical Laboratory. He fitted me out with a supply of polar clothing of the kind which had been worn by his own Antarctic expedition. When I arrived home, exactly forty-eight hours after receiving the telegram, I had seventeen hours left to sailing time.

Next morning I embarked at Glasgow's Broomielaw. My father and a dozen or so of my family and closest friends came with me on the *Grampian* as far as the Tail of the Bank at Greenock, then went ashore in a tender, waving goodbye until they were blotted out by sweeping rain squalls. I was alone with my thoughts, and with all the time in the world to reflect on what I had undertaken and what it might mean for myself and for those I was leaving behind. Dr Bruce, sensing the fears of a mother who had devoted her life unsparingly to her large family, had done his best to reassure her that I would be in no more danger from the Arctic ice than I would be dodging chimney pots and roof slates in a Glasgow storm. Whatever her thoughts, she kept them to herself. I wonder whether she found any consolation in the heroic lines published in my honour by the local newspaper:

To The Far, Far North

I pen me a meed for a youth of the rarest,
Who spent his young years on Radnor's sweet mound,
Ere reaching the hill-top where science blooms fairest,
And yields to her climbers rich fruits which abound.
    My meed I'll raise
    To bless his days,
And safeguard where danger is found.

Far, far to the North in the lone Arctic regions,
Stern duty has led him its gloom to dispel
To tap its resources in units or legions,
And then back to homeland the story to tell;
    May joy attend,
    And heaven defend,
Nor may they depart from 'All's Well'.

Blow gently, ye winds o'er the waste, in soft billows,
O kiss him with comfort and guide well his prow;
Know ye there are loved ones who press not their pillows,
Until at the Throne for his weal they do bow;
    Blow gently gales,
    Just fill their sails,
Lend a charm to the fervent vow.

Radnor felt honoured to learn that her offspring,
Had reached the high altitude few could attain;
Right glad was her heart and sincere as the offering,
She trusted that mankind more knowledge might gain;
    May health and strength
    Be at his length,
To rove in that unexplored main.

Auld Monk

    I was busy being seasick for the first two days and then settled down to enjoy the comforts and pleasures of an Atlantic voyage – as well as the dangers; we ran into dense fog in the same area where the *Titanic* had sunk just over a year earlier. The conditions were identical – all around us icebergs of every shape and size. We could only occasionally see them, but we knew how close they were from the echo of the ship's siren

9

reverberating from the masses of ice. For days we steamed 'Dead Slow Ahead', and once a sudden stopping and immediate reversal of the engines sent a staggering shudder through the ship, and those of us on deck could faintly glimpse the huge iceberg as it drifted majestically past. I had not expected to meet ice so soon!

After we reached Montreal I travelled to Toronto where I was met by a member of the Dominion Meteorological Service. I was delighted to learn from him that the Meteorological Service was going to pay me a salary of $60 a month – double the £90 a year I was earning as a teacher in Scotland. But he started my first feelings of doubt when he told me that the reason I had been hired as meteorologist as well as magnetician was because no one in the Meteorological Service was willing to be associated with Stefansson's expedition. It was the first of many hints I was to receive as the weeks went by that not everyone shared the faith of Admiral Peary and popular Canadian newspaper writers in the suitability of Stefansson as an expedition leader.

But I shook off my doubts and settled down to enjoy three enchanting weeks at the Magnetic Observatory, near Agincourt, fourteen miles from Toronto. I familiarized myself with all the equipment I expected to be using during the next four years in much less agreeable surroundings. Then I was off on the long train journey across Canada to Vancouver on the Pacific coast, and from there by steamer to Victoria, the capital of Vancouver Island. This was the Canadian port nearest to the Alaska frontier, and it was from here that we would sail out into the North Pacific, round the Aleutian Islands and up the coast of Alaska to its chief port, Nome, mecca of fur traders, gold prospectors and other seekers after fortune, adventure or just a living in the far north. From Nome we would sail through the Bering Strait between Alaska and Siberia, then follow the Alaskan coast round its northernmost point to where it meets the northernmost coast of Canada.

It was 6 am on Monday, 1 June 1913, when I arrived in Victoria, feeling a little lost. I had no idea where the staff of the expedition were staying, so I made my way to the Navy Yard at Esquimalt, where our ship, the *Karluk*, was being fitted out. It was eight o'clock before Dr Alistair Mackay and Diamond Jenness, one of our anthropologists, turned up and took me aboard. The *Karluk* was a twenty-year-old whaling ship, whose overhaul was said to be costing $10,000. As we were passing above the engine-room a voice rang out from below, 'Hello, Glesca!' It was John Munro, the chief engineer, who hailed from Inveraray, in Argyll, but had become a Canadian citizen. Mackay and Jenness took me to breakfast at the James Bay Hotel, where I met James Murray, from Edinburgh, at forty-six years of age the oldest man in the expedition, and, like Mackay, a veteran of the Shackleton Antarctic expedition. Dr Anderson, our second-in-command, was there, too, and he and Murray had their wives with them. There was no sign of Stefansson.

The people of Victoria treated us like heroes. When we were not busy loading supplies on the ship, we were being lunched and dined by clubs and societies and private citizens who queued up to offer us hospitality. But as the days passed I began to have misgivings about the management of the expedition. There was still no sign of Stefansson. As I got to know more of my colleagues I had the feeling that all was not as well with things as our leader made out in his frequent press statements. There were rumblings of discontent among the scientific staff, and real doubts were being expressed about the plan of campaign – or lack of it – by those members who had been seconded from the Geological Survey of the Canadian Department of Mines. There were many points that the men wished to discuss with the leader, but although we were scheduled to sail on 10 June, Stefansson did not put in an appearance until the seventh. At once he held a conference which lasted five hours. I was not sufficiently in touch with the plans to appreciate the significance of all the points that were raised, but I was left in no doubt that there were many uncertainties hanging over our venture. There was, for instance, the matter of the *Karluk*. My knowledge of the preparation of ships for exploration was not based on experience, but from my reading and from many meetings with polar men in Edinburgh, I knew the meticulous care that had to be given to such preparations. The *Karluk* had been purchased by Stefansson after she had been laid up for several years during a slump in the whaling industry. Although she had been in the whaling service, she had been built for the fishing industry in the Aleutian Islands (*karluk* is the Aleutian word for fish). Her bow had been strengthened for whaling in the polar seas, but as our skipper, Captain Robert Bartlett, put it in *The Last Voyage of the Karluk*, 'she had neither the strength to sustain pressure, nor the engine power to force her way through loose ice'. Captain Bartlett knew what he was talking about. He had skippered Peary's *Roosevelt*, which was specially built to withstand ice pressure, as was Nansen's *Fram*, which could slide up on top of the floes instead of being crushed by them

Captain Bartlett was Stefansson's second choice as a skipper. He had wanted Captain C. T. Pedersen of San Francisco, but Pedersen was afraid of losing his American citizenship if he took command of a Canadian expedition, so Captain Bartlett (also an American citizen, though born in Newfoundland) received one of those last-minute telegrams, like mine, and arrived in Victoria at the end of May to take over the *Karluk*. What had been done in the way of refitting her for the trials to come I just did not know, but not a great deal could have been achieved in the time available – little more than three months.

Another worry was the recruitment of the crew. They were not chosen by Captain Bartlett, for they were all there by the time he arrived. A government official declared that they had been 'picked up along the coast'. One of the crew told me that the week before he came to Victoria he had been stranded on the beach at Antofagasta, with only a singlet and a pair of canvas trousers to his name. One was a confirmed drug addict, who carried around a pocket-sized case with half-a-dozen phials of drugs and two hypodermic syringes; another suffered from venereal disease; and in spite of orders that no liquor was to be carried, at least two smuggled supplies on board. There were a few fine types whom I came to admire greatly. The most outstanding was a Scot, Sandy Anderson, who signed on as second officer, but whom Bartlett promoted to Mate almost as soon as he arrived at Victoria, after dismissing the first officer for incompetence. Sandy had just got his second mate's ticket and was only twenty.

I had no reason to doubt the crew's seamanship (and events were to prove them completely competent in this respect), but I had grave doubts in many cases about the other qualities which would be necessary for harmonious living in the kind of circumstances which might face us in the north. Of course the plan was that after establishing the winter base, the *Karluk* should, if possible, be sent south for the winter, and it may be that in choosing a crew, whoever was responsible did not expect them to have to face the stresses and strains that did, in fact, occur. In the *Montreal*

Star, 1 May 1913, Stefansson was reported as saying, 'I am going to employ only British subjects wherever British subjects are available. Meanwhile I have ten times as many British volunteers as can be taken. All the positions, even those of cabin-boy, cook, carpenter and foremost hands could be filled by British subjects of university education and social position who are willing to serve without pay.'

There were certainly no university degrees among the crew. The scientific staff were not all British subjects. Only five were Canadians; three were from Scotland, two from the United States, one from Australia, one from New Zealand, one from Denmark, one from Norway and one from France. All except Stefansson's secretary, Burt McConnell, were graduates, from eleven different universities. All of us, staff and crew, worked amicably enough side by side to get the *Karluk* ready for sailing. We were only a week behind schedule when we finally got under way on Wednesday, 17 June. We steamed round Esquimalt Harbour to cheers from the entire Canadian Pacific Fleet, lined up on deck and filling the rigging. Good luck signals were hoisted, sirens wailed, and we were off in a glorious sunset. Stefansson, Dr Anderson, James Murray and the ladies escorted us in a motor launch. They were going to follow later by the regular mail steamer and join us at Nome. Before they left, Stefansson bought a second ship, the *Alaska*, to serve as a supply vessel.

3   *A Stormy Meeting*

After a stormy voyage, during which we were bedevilled by fog, engine failure and broken hawsers (five times), and spent most of our time shovelling coal from the crowded deck into the bunkers below, we arrived at Nome on 8 July and dropped anchor about a mile from the 'Golden Strand'. There were men panning for gold along the beach as we went ashore next morning. Stefansson arrived just after us, and we found that he had bought a third ship, the *Mary Sachs*, to add to our expanding fleet. Tons of additional supplies had arrived on the mail steamer *Victoria* with Stefansson; tons more were being bought in Nome. All this had to be loaded on to our three vessels, and large quantities had to be unloaded from the *Karluk* and transferred to the other two ships. The perfect method would of course have been to distribute the loads according to the planned destinations and functions of the different ships, but this was not done. There seemed to be no one in charge to direct operations. In the haste and confusion, when anyone asked where this or that should go, the answer was always the same: 'We'll sort that out at Herschel Island.' How familiar that phrase was to become. Herschel Island was the place near the Alaskan–Canadian north-coast frontier where all the ships were to rendezvous before the different parties went to their planned locations.

Stefansson outlined the plan in his book, *The Friendly Arctic* (p. 51):

My plan was that, with Murray in command of her, the *Sachs* should act in a measure as a tender, carrying supplies for Dr Anderson towards Coronation Gulf or doing similar errands for Bartlett and the *Karluk* if that became necessary. She was to hold herself ready whenever needed. In her spare time, which I hoped would be considerable, the *Sachs* was to cruise about in the triangle between Herschel Island and Cape Kellett, venturing as far as she cared northwestward into the Beaufort Sea, but always keeping in this comparatively ice-free district. For, although she was seaworthy and staunch in every other way, she was incapacitated for too close contact with the ice through having two propellors. An unexpected increase of cargo at Nome had compelled us to buy the *Sachs*, in spite of the twin-propellor drawback, as the only craft available.

Some of the staff were extremely dissatisfied with the plans, especially James Murray, the veteran of the Shackleton Expedition. He and Kenneth Chipman were detailed to ask Stefansson for a staff conference and it took place on 10 July. We argued about the problems involved in the basic plan to set up two main parties: one, the Southern Party, to operate under Dr Anderson in the area around Coronation Gulf and the islands off the Canadian north coast; the other, the Northern Party, to head out into the great unknown under the leadership of Stefansson. I was to serve in both parties.

An excerpt from my diary, Thursday, 10 July, reads:

This [conference] came about 8 pm and lasted until 12.45 am, discussing many important matters. As a result we gathered the assurance that all things are satisfactory so far as the Southern Party is concerned, but the same cannot be said of the Northern Party. Stefansson seemed to resent our attitude in endeavouring to obtain details as to provisions for food, clothing, facilities for work, etc. and he went the length of telling Murray, when he asked what provision was being made for fur clothing, that the question was impertinent. He told us that he thought our whole conduct in calling for a meeting seemed to imply a lack of confidence in our leader, and altogether failed to recognize that we all had an undeniable right to assure ourselves that every regard was being had for our protection. ... The uncertainty of the movements of the Northern Party made me raise the question of my own position and that of Wilkins, since Stefansson desired us to come north after a year in the south. We frankly put it to him that we would make no attempt to leave the Southern Party until we received definite word as to the location of the Northern Party, and until means of absolutely safe transport was assured us. The probability is that, in the light of present arrangements, we shall both remain in the south for the whole time; we shall take no foolhardy risks, and in this we have the unanimous support of our fellows. The position of the Northern Party is serious and no one would be surprised should Murray resign.

I was so worried that I wrote a letter to one of my closest friends, who lived about 300 yards from my home in Clydebank, and added a very long postscript. It was dated 12 July 1913, Nome: 'PS I have some very serious matters to write upon now, and I wish you to keep this part strictly private, and also to do me the favour of carefully preserving it for my return in case of emergency. It concerns the management and equipment of the expedition, and you will appreciate these requests when you read what follows. . . .' I then gave a detailed account of the meeting with Stefansson, underlining my concern about the plans for the Northern Party:

Our first information was that the *Karluk* was to proceed along the 141st meridian, and if no new land was found, a base was to be established on Prince Patrick Island, from which explorations were to be made into the unknown. The *Karluk* was to return immediately or, if that was not possible, then the following summer, for provisions. Stefansson has, however, disclosed in exclusive paper interviews and also in our hearing, that the *Karluk* would proceed as far as she could, and would probably be frozen in; and in this case, she would certainly be crushed and sink. . . . Stefansson had declared that every member of the scientific staff recognized that his life was a secondary matter compared with the scientific work, which was not only untrue, but in direct opposition to the government's instructions. No satisfactory explanation of these matters or of the plans for the Northern Party was given.

With regard to the position of Wilkins and myself, we distinctly stated that we would not undertake the journey to the north . . . until we received definite word that a Northern base had been established and that one of our ships was available to take us north; and in deference to the general wish of our fellows, who considered Stefansson's original instructions suicidal for us, Stefansson agreed. This makes our position perfectly satisfactory, and it is most probable that we will remain with the southern party. . . .

The affairs of the Southern Party are entirely satisfactory and we are in the hands of a capable leader, Dr Anderson, in whom we have perfect confidence.

There was a lot of anxious letter-writing after that meeting with Stefansson. I have copies of letters which Chipman and O'Neill, who had been seconded to the expedition from the Geological Survey of the Canadian Department of Mines, wrote to their director.

Chipman wrote:

We had the second of our general conferences. Murray and I were spokesmen and raised such questions as food supply, clothing, travel, equipment, where base is to be, coordination of work, etc. There was nothing new! I raised these

16

questions twice in Ottawa and his [Stefansson's] answers are the same now as then. He, however, informs us that we had no business to ask these questions, that we should have confidence in him.

O'Neill wrote:

Stefansson has been having his hands full trying to pacify the fellows of the Northern Party. He is close-mouthed as the devil about his plans and they want it definitely settled that a base will be established to give them something to fall back on if the ship gets pinched, which seems more than likely from what I hear. At a mass meeting this bunch broached his lordship for certain pieces of information. Murray was rather too aggressive, I think, and Stefansson did not give him much satisfaction. The deficient water supply on the *Karluk* was worrying Murray considerably as well as getting caught in the ice and no base to fall back on.

The two days following the conference were a hectic scramble to finish the loading of the ships, and as the activity increased so did the confusion. Again and again the cry went up: 'We'll sort things out at Herschel Island.' Not even the most pessimistic of us thought for a moment that some of us would never see Herschel Island. Stefansson ordered the *Karluk* to leave Nome on 13 July for Port Clarence, further up the coast. Malloch, Beuchat, Jenness, Mamen, Mackay and I were to go along and wait at Port Clarence for the rest of the staff to arrive in the other two ships. When we got on board the *Karluk* there was utter confusion on deck, not a square inch of vacant space, disorderly piles of stores scattered around, giving the appearance of a neglected junk-yard. As Stefansson wrote in *The Friendly Arctic*:

Our 250-ton *Karluk* was carrying more than she should below decks and on deck she had 150 tons with which she would never have been allowed to sail had there been at the port of Nome rigid inspectors unwilling to except an exploring vessel from the rules that are supposed to promote the safety of ships at sea. She was so deep in the water with heavy cargo that her decks were nearly awash.

A violent storm hit Nome after we left and we had a week extra to wait in Port Clarence before the *Alaska* and *Mary Sachs* arrived. Jenness and I spent most of the time trying to restore order in the hold of the *Karluk*. In the end I had still not located some of my boxes of instruments, and the Skipper promised, with a grin, that he would have the hold cleared and stowed again 'when we reach Herschel Island'. Meanwhile the *Mary Sachs* tied up alongside with a bewildering array of tins, sledges, fur clothing, dogs, and an Eskimo woman, who was to act as seamstress. Another ship, the *Corwin*, arrived with Stefansson, Mr and Mrs Murray, George Wilkins (the photographer), two lady stenographers and twenty-eight dogs – the pick of the kennels of Scotty Allan, the finest breeder in all Alaska. The dogs were somehow transferred to the *Karluk* and added their yowling, yapping and scrapping to the general confusion. If anyone could now tell what we had on board, or where it was, well – we would find out when we got to. ...

On Friday, 26 July 1913, we sailed from Port Clarence for the rendezvous at Herschel Island. The following people were on the *Karluk*:

Crew
Robert A. Bartlett, *Master*
Alex ('Sandy') Anderson, *First Officer*
Charles Barker, *Second Officer*
John Munro, *Chief Engineer*
Robert Williamson, *Second Engineer*
John Brady, *Seaman*
G. Breddy, *Fireman*
Ernest Chafe ('Charlie'), *Messroom Boy*
A. King (real name 'Golightly'), *Seaman*
Fred Maurer, *Fireman*
S. Stanley Morris, *Seaman*
Robert Templeman, *Cook and Steward*
H. Williams ('Clam'), *Seaman*

Scientific Staff
Vilhjalmur Stefansson, *Commander*
Diamond Jenness, *Anthropologist*
Burt McConnell, *Secretary*
George H. Wilkins, *Photographer*
Henri Beauchat, *Anthropologist*
Alistair Forbes Mackay, *Surgeon*
William L. McKinlay, *Magnetician and Meteorologist*

George Malloch, *Geologist*
Bjarne Mamen, *Assistant Topographer*
James Murray, *Oceanographer*

And the ship's cat, Nigeraurak ('little black one'), shanghaied by one of the crew when we were in Victoria.

Anderson, Chipman, Cox, Johanssen and O'Neill were on the *Alaska* and the *Mary Sachs* (the ladies had gone back on the *Corwin*) and we were all to be sorted out, like the stores, at Herschel Island. Surely Stefansson must have realized, even if greenhorns like me did not, that there was at least an outside chance that the rendezvous at Herschel Island would never take place? Yet no attempt was made to have the right people on the right ships before we left Port Clarence, far less the right equipment. According to Stefansson himself, . . . 'We had on board several men who had no business to be there. James Murray was one. . . . I had decided to put him in charge of the *Mary Sachs*.'

Yet here he was on the *Karluk*. So was all his oceanographical equipment. Apparently this was to be sorted out of the conglomeration in the hold before we got to Herschel Island, so that it could be transferred with Murray to the *Sachs*. I should not have been on the *Karluk* either. Again, in Stefansson's own words: 'McKinlay should have been elsewhere. If he were to be in the *Karluk* he should of course have had with him all his magnetic equipment, some of which was now on the *Alaska*. The *Karluk* also carried the two anthropologists, Beuchat and Jenness, who, to quote Stefansson again, 'had been taken aboard because the *Karluk* was not only the safest but the swiftest conveyance for Herschel Island', where they were to be landed to study the Eskimos. Of course, as Stefansson put it, 'Their equipment was naturally most of it aboard the *Alaska*.'

Heaven help us all if we failed to reach Herschel Island!

4   *Caught in the Ice*

We steamed near the coast for a time after leaving Port Clarence, and we were passing Tin City when a rowing boat came towards us with a telephone message. It was from an aviator called Fowler, and he wanted us to take him and his plane part of our way north, so that he could fly back. There was not even room for a toy plane among the clutter of coal, sledges and dogs on our decks, so Stefansson had to say no, but I sometimes wonder whether, if we had taken him along, Mr Fowler might have become the first airman in history to bring help to a stranded Arctic expedition.

We crossed the Arctic Circle at 4 am on 27 July and celebrated at dinner with a bottle of wine which had been presented to Stefansson by a friend for this occasion. Next morning we ran into dense fog, with a rising northwest wind and a mounting sea. Quickly we progressed from 'fresh breeze', through 'strong breeze' to 'light gale' and 'moderate gale'. Once through the Bering Strait and into the open Arctic Ocean we felt the full impact of the screeching wind. *Karluk* behaved magnificently; she rose to every wave like a duck. Whatever defects she had she was proving herself a fine sea-boat; she seemed to be in her element, which was more than could be said for most of the landlubbers on board. Every one of my colleagues was down with sea-sickness, but I had long since developed my sea-legs and had not the slightest vestige of squeamishness. I went up on deck, enjoying every minute of the storm. Everything movable was being tossed about. The poor dogs huddled on the fo'c'sle-head, soaked and miserable. We decided to move as many as possible to the after-deck, but the mixing of different teams caused dog fights which made the operation extremely hazardous. Although the engines were stretched to their utmost, we were making little or no headway, at the most three-quarters of a knot, with about the same leeway. In fact we were at a standstill. After the evening meal, at which I was the only non-crew member present, I went on deck again and remained there until midnight, sharing the watch with Sandy Anderson on the bridge. He allowed me to stay on condition that he lashed me to a stanchion while the gale reached its peak and waves swept over our heads, high though we were on the bridge. When I had made the midnight reading of the few instruments to which I had access, I went below to the galley, had several mugs of tea with the changing watch and turned in, feeling on top of the world.

At ten o'clock the next night we anchored near Point Hope, about a mile off the village of Tigerak, with its Eskimo settlement, mission and whaling station. Here Stefansson bought skins and boots and hired two Eskimos, Paujurak and Asatshuk (Jimmy and Jerry) as hunters and dog drivers. By now we had a favourable fore and aft breeze, increasing in force, and the *Karluk* set off from Point Hope under sail, scudding along at eight or nine knots. That night my watch with Sandy was much more comfortable, but now it was bitterly cold, and we could 'smell' that ice was not far off. The temperature during the night fell well below freezing point. By forenoon it was 27° Fahrenheit. The wind was bitterly cold, out of the north, and soon it began to snow – on 1 August! I was on the bridge helping with the steering, which, owing to the breakdown of the compass in the wheelhouse, involved knocking down to the men in the wheelhouse below and reading them the course from the Kelvin compass on the bridge. I was muffled up in winter clothing against the wind, which was still blowing strongly, though the swell on the water was gradually subsiding – another sign that ice was in the offing.

Early next morning I saw my first ice-blink – a long, white band stretching all along the distant water-horizon. At 6 am the second mate reported ice on the port bow, and we could see the extensive ice pack from the bridge. An hour later it was on the port beam, about a mile and a half away. About 11 am it was reported to starboard, and shortly thereafter land was sighted on the starboard bow. Captain Bartlett scanned the pack from the crow's nest to see if a lead (opening) could be found in the ice, but after several attempts to get through at what looked likely places, we had to give up and steam south again. We made another attempt to penetrate the pack next morning, 3 August, but again we failed. We were just off Point Belcher when a change of wind began to ease the pack away from the land, and at last we were able to go ahead, pushing through the loose ice fairly easily. We were on a north-east course for Point Barrow, seventy-five miles away. If we had been a few days earlier we would have had open water all the way to Point Barrow, but those days of delay at Port Clarence were going to cost us dearly.

Now the pack was beginning to close again. As we nudged our way through, we passed a herd of walrus on the port beam, and two or three of them came tumbling about quite near the ship. Then, from the crow's nest, Captain sighted a polar bear on the ice about five hundred yards off. Mamen and Jenness had a few shots at him, but all of them missed and he was off like an arrow at an astonishing speed. Another appeared not far from the bow, and this time the captain had a go. By the time we had rushed up on deck the huge carcass was floating in a lead, with a floe between him and the ship. A whaleboat was lowered and soon he was on board, and the Eskimos began skinning and cutting up. He was heavy and fat, a welcome addition to our larder, both for men and dogs.

August third. From 8 pm till midnight we had some very hard going. The pack was becoming more and more heavy and closing up rapidly. Our frail *Karluk* took many a hard knock, the worst one when the man at the wheel, echoing the captain's 'Hard a starboard!' from the crow's nest, inexplicably swung us hard to port, and we crashed bow-on to a heavy floe. By now the ice was so heavily packed that we were at a complete standstill, hemmed in tightly all round.

I was fascinated by the scene. The ice was much broken up and rough, with scarcely a level patch of any great extent. The multitude of hummocks of varying size and height had weathered throughout the summer so that their surfaces were clear of snow and all their edges had been smoothed and rounded. Their shapes were infinite in variety and they gleamed and glistened in every conceivable shade of blue. It was like being in some gigantic sculptor's-yard, stacked as far as the eye could see with glistening marble blocks cut in a million fantastic shapes. As people do when confronted with great sculpture, I had the irresistible urge to touch as well as look. We left the ship and cavorted about on the ice for hours.

There was little or no darkness in the Arctic at this time of year and it was 4 am before we climbed back on board and went to our bunks.

August fourth. The ship was wedged in as tightly as ever. The wind was still blowing on to the Alaskan coast and as long as this continued there was no hope of the ice's grip loosening. Stefansson decided to cross the ice by sledge to Point Barrow, about twenty-five miles away. He set off after dinner with the doctor and the Eskimos, who were to bring back the dogs and the sledge. The Eskimos returned about midnight and told us that the going, over broken and uneven ice, had been extremely difficult and dangerous. The doctor had fallen into water and was on the point of exhaustion by the time they reached the land ice. He and Stefansson were going on to the trading settlement at Cape Smythe, and it looked as if we would be joining them there soon, because although we were still firmly stuck in the ice, we were moving with the pack, drifting towards the coast at a rate varying between three and eight miles a day.

August sixth. At long last the captain managed to get us free of the ice and under steam again. It was 2 am, but five minutes later the steering broke down again. To be without steering in the middle of an ice pack was a serious business, and it took two hours to mend the trouble. We were able to go ahead again, but soon the closing ice forced us to a standstill. We were about a mile from the settlement at Cape Smythe and in the afternoon the doctor came across the ice, followed by about thirty-six Eskimos carrying purchases Stefansson had made at the trading post – furs, two kayaks and two *umiaks* (skin boats).

Stefansson had engaged five more Eskimos to join the expedition. There was a family of four – Kuraluk, the father, who was signed on as a hunter; Kiruk, his wife, soon known to us all as Auntie, who was to be the party's seamstress; and their two daughters, Helen, aged eleven, and Mugpi, who was three. We cleared coal, casks and timber from the alleyway alongside the ship's laboratory to make living quarters for the little family. The fifth Eskimo, a widow called Kataktovik, moved in with Paujuruk and Asatshuk. While all this activity was going on Stefansson came aboard with another addition to the party, John Hadley, an employee of the Cape Smythe Trading Company. We had no idea why Hadley was joining us. Stefansson explained in *The Friendly Arctic*:

There were many reasons why I wanted him. For one thing, all my men were

23

new in the Arctic except Bartlett, and Bartlett came from a part of the Arctic where conditions are so fundamentally different from what they are around Alaska that I felt the need of at least one man with whom I could talk over local conditions with the certainty that he had the knowledge necessary to criticize my own ideas and give opinions of value. ... His experience was of all sorts. He had been trapper and trader, and a whaler, both on board ships and with Eskimos in their skin boats.

In his book Captain Bartlett described Hadley as:

a man between fifty-five and sixty years old, who had for a long time been in charge of the whaling station at Cape Smythe. ... Mr Hadley had resigned his position to go east to Banks Land and establish a trading station of his own, chiefly to get fox-skins by barter with the Eskimos. As we were on our way to Herschel Island, now was Mr Hadley's chance to get to his destination, for at Herschel Island he could be transferred to the *Mary Sachs* or the *Alaska* when they reached there, and so go east in the direction of Banks Land. ...

So now we were thirty, and the seeds of dissension were being sown all the time. The crew got very annoyed when they saw Stefansson issuing the Eskimos with sheepskin coats, parkas, makluks and other polar gear; the Eskimos were already wearing their own warm outfits when they came aboard, yet neither the crew nor the staff had been issued with any Arctic clothing at all. There was some wild talk among the crew, and some of them spoke quite openly of deserting at the first opportunity. But there was little chance of that. We were now firmly in the grip of the ice, and were being carried helplessly northwest, stern first. This was not at all what had been planned. We were supposed to be steaming northeast to that magic meeting-place, Herschel Island. Instead we were drifting into the icy graveyard of many a whaling ship, at the rate of at least a mile per hour, and were already out of sight of land.

5 *Goodbye Stefansson*

On 9 August the ice relaxed its hold and we were able to nose our way slowly to the east. Indeed, at times we had enough open water to allow us to go full speed ahead, and two more such days would have seen us at Herschel Island. But the ice was slowly tightening up again. Little or no steering could be done by the compass; the look-out in the 'barrell' followed the leads, to keep clear of the floes, with the result that the course was continually changing, and at times we appeared to be going around in circles.

Captain Barlett used all his skill in trying to push eastward. He was giving up hope of any exploring work before winter finally set in, but he was desperately anxious to get to Herschel Island. We got as far as Lion Reef when we again came to a halt. The following day the ice slackened to the northeast, and we moved a little, but the ice was packed close inshore.

Captain Bartlett wrote: 'August 12. About 8 pm we were stopped by a large unbroken sheet of ice. This was very similar to the ice which I have seen in Melville Bay on the west Greenland coast; it was part of the past season's ice. Seldom over a foot thick, it was honey-combed with water-holes; the *Roosevelt* could have ploughed through it, but the *Karluk* was powerless to do so.'

Captain Bartlett examined the stem of the ship and found that already two of the brass stem-plates were gone and several bolts loosened on those that remained. All the *Karluk* could do was to follow open lanes and go where they led – as Stefansson described it, 'threading our way between the ice cakes and occasionally ramming to break a way'.

Soon it was very evident that we had reached our eastern limit. Snow began to fall, the temperature dropped to 17° Fahrenheit and young ice began to form in the small openings between the floes, cementing the pack into one impenetrable mass. We were motionless; so was the ice. Then, in the last week of August, the ice started moving in a solid pack, slowly, to the west, taking us with it about twenty miles a day, sometimes faster. Sometimes we could see an open lead, but always too far off to be of any use to us. Stefansson called Beuchat, Jenness, Murray, Wilkins and myself into his cabin one evening to discuss the advisability of our going ashore before we drifted any farther away from it. Murray and I were quickly ruled out because of the weight of our gear. Wilkins' position, too, was doubtful because of his equipment. This left Jenness and Beuchat, who, of course could do none of their work on board; their place as anthropologists was among the Eskimos. Stefansson left the decision to them and next day they told him they were willing to go.

The preparations for their departure gave rise to the usual confusion. Stefansson wanted a particular type of tent, but two-days' search in the hold proved fruitless. By 26 August everything appeared to be ready and their departure was fixed for the next day; but when that arrived the weather was very cheerless with heavy snowfall. 'I don't like you leaving in this weather,' said Stefansson. 'The ice is rotten, and the snow will cover it up so you can't see where you're going. Tomorrow perhaps.' Next day the Eskimos were afraid of the travelling conditions, so there was another postponement. Stefansson gave Jenness $800 for travelling expenses, and a letter to the Northwest Mounted Police at Herschel Island. On the way they were to call at Flaxman Island to ask for news of the *Alaska* and *Mary Sachs*, and leave a message for their commanders. Stefansson also gave the two men a letter, authorizing them to act independently of the expedition if circumstances warranted it, and typed instructions making them an independent unit responsible to the Naval Service. As well as the $800 cash they took a cheque for $200, with authority to engage as many Eskimos as they required. They were to do whatever work they considered advisable, always bearing in mind that they must attach themselves as soon as possible to the Southern Party. He also gave Jenness orders to telegraph a news story to the *New York Times*.

It was 29 August before they got away. They had two sledges with seven dogs to each, the first loaded with provisions and equipment, the second with an *umiak*. Both were too heavily laden. Kataktovik was to go with them all the way, and they were to be escorted part of the way by Jimmy and Jerry, and three or four of the staff. They made heavy going, for the ice was well covered with snow, which made it difficult to pick a good trail. One sledge broke through a hole and was immersed to the handles, and the *umiak* suffered severe damage. After several hours hard work they had covered two miles by trail, but not much more than a mile from the ship in a direct line. They stopped for a meal—a cold one, for they had lost part of their Primus stove.

After dinner on board, Stefansson and Hadley went off to catch them up with mail to be sent from Herschel Island. When they saw the state of the ice, the damaged *umiak*, and the overloaded sledges, Stefansson decided to call off the attempt. Some of the stores were cached, and the more valuable parts were taken back to the ship. It took them only twenty minutes to return over the distance which had taken them over two hours on the outward journey. Beuchat fell through the ice and had to be put into the *umiak* and carried back.

Now followed weeks of monotony and frustration. Murray alone of the scientific staff was able to carry on with the work he had come to do. He worked assiduously, day in, day out, dredging and collecting from all depths of the ocean. One single haul brought in some polychoete worms, a sea mouse, some ophyurids, two species of gastropods, two species of lamelli-branchiata (one yellow, one white), some holothurians, cirripedia, polyzoa (lace coral), a pecten, some schizopods, a shrimp with exceptionally long legs, some small red amphipods. . . . When he was not busy in the ice-holes, he was busy in the laboratory, preserving his specimens in bottles, labelling them, writing notes. I wish I had thought of duplicating his notes, so that some record might have survived of many months of unremitting labour.

The rest of us had to relieve the monotony as best we could. There were some days when open lanes of water gave us the opportunity to go hunting for birds and seals, but we were not very good at it. When we killed birds they would fall in the water where we could not retrieve them; if we shot a seal it invariably sank. The Eskimos, on the other hand, were highly skilled in the use of the *manak*, which consisted of a lead weight of about six pounds at the end of a long line; a foot or so above the weight a cluster of four large hooks was fixed. Holding the line coiled like a lariat, the Eskimo cast the weight a little beyond the seal and then pulled the line. The hooks caught in the carcass, which could then be dragged to the edge of the ice.

Thanks to the Eskimos, especially Kuraluk, we now had seal meat at every meal. It was dark in appearance, smelled strong and tasted fishy. The liver, particularly of a young seal, was extremely tasty, and one sometimes got a really succulent steak. Seal steak-and-kidney pie was on our menu once a week.

The steady drift of the ice-pack continued, but for some days around the middle of September we were at a standstill, locked to the far distant land in a wedge of ice. According to the captain, Stefansson had finally made up his mind that all hope of progress for this year was ended. He was becoming worried about the prospects of getting sufficient fresh meat in the area, although our Eskimos were building up a stock which we had no difficulty in keeping fresh. The entire ice pack around us was a huge natural refrigerator. But Stefansson was not satisfied, and on the evening of 19 September he announced that he was going ashore on a caribou hunt, with Wilkins, McConnell, and the two Eskimos, Jimmy and Jerry. This came as a surprise to some of us, because not long before he had told us that in northern Alaska the caribou (North American reindeer) was practically extinct. A little later that evening he added Jenness to the party 'to give him a chance to begin his study of the Eskimo'. I have never ceased to wonder why he did not include Beuchat for the same reason.

He left the captain a long letter, giving detailed instructions about setting out beacons and flags on the ice to facilitate his return to the ship:

If it becomes practicable, send off Mamen and Malloch for surveying purposes. McKinlay should accompany them for the purpose of establishing magnetic stations in connection with Malloch's survey, Malloch locating the stations for McKinlay, so as to save unnecessary duplication of instruments. Except for some especial reason, the Eskimo woman, Kiruk, should be kept sewing boots of the winter service type – deer-legs, using ugrug soles.

It is likely [the letter finished] that we shall be back to the ship in ten days if no accident happens.

Stefansson did not return to the ship in ten days. He did not return ever. Two days after he left, the wind which had been blowing moderately from the east increased to a gale, and next morning the ice had split between the ship and the shore. We were being carried away from the land in the grip of the gale-swept ice-pack, moving west at the rate of thirty miles a day, leaving an ever widening expanse of Arctic sea between us and our leader.

6   *The Man Who Lost His Ship*

It seems inconceivable to me that Stefansson should have left his ship when he did. He had already made up his mind, as he explained in his book, that one of four things was likely to happen to the *Karluk*:

1. With a mild east-wind the ice would break outside the *Karluk* and move westward offshore, leaving her 'unmoved and unconcerned'.
2. The east-wind might persist for a long time or develop into a strong gale, which would push the outside ice against the shore ice, 'crushing the ship or failing to crush her exactly according to luck'.
3. A light west-wind might break the ice outside, leaving her again unaffected.
4. If it were a strong gale it might carry her to the east, grinding along in the pack, leaving her afloat or sinking her, 'again according to fortune'.

This last possibility must have been the one he considered most probable, because he wrote that as soon as we started drifting with the pack: '[I] made up my mind that the *Karluk* was not to move under her own power again, and that we were in for a voyage such as that of the *Jeannette* or the *Fram*, drifting for years, if we had the luck to remain unbroken, eventually coming out towards the Atlantic, either we or our wreckage.'

Yet on 20 September he was prepared to risk leaving us stuck out there on the ice, on the chance that 'if any party were to go ashore temporarily they could always get back to the *Karluk*; for they would find her either just where they left her or to the east. It did not occur to us that she could be carried off, unbroken, far to the westward.'

He and his party were about ten miles away, not on the mainland, but on Amauliktok, the westernmost of the Jones Islands, about four miles off the coast, when the gale struck which broke our ice pack away from the land. Stefansson called it 'the worst storm for that season which I have ever seen in the north'; and when it was over 'the *Karluk* was gone; we did not know whither, or whether she still survived. There was no sense in searching for her by sled, for there was vastly more water than ice, so we went on to the mainland.'

When the ice hardened, Stefansson decided to make his way west along the coast in the hope of overtaking the *Karluk*: 'The chances were that the ice holding her had followed the coast towards Barrow.' At Cape Smythe he learned that none of his ships had got anywhere near Herschel Island. The *Alaska* and *Mary Sachs* were reported safe at Collinson Point (the *Mary Sachs* later broke down and was abandoned at Cape Kellett; her commander, Captain Bernard, and Charles Thomsen perished in 1916 trying to take supplies to Stefansson across the ice) but there was no news of the *Karluk*, apart from Eskimo accounts of a ship answering to the *Karluk's* description, which had been seen for two or three days before vanishing into the fog.

Stefansson commented:

It was especially unfortunate for us that to the *Karluk*, believed safest of all our ships, we had entrusted the most valued part of our cargo. One of the main things I wanted to do that next spring on the sledge journey over the Beaufort Sea was to take soundings, and most of our sounding equipment was on the *Karluk*. The *Sachs* and *Alaska* had chronometers for their own use, but the ones intended for sledge exploration were on the *Karluk*. The men of adventurous disposition and special qualifications, whom I had meant for my companions on exploratory journeys, were also there, along with the good dogs purchased in Nome, and the sledges and sledge material which could not be duplicated even at Cape Smythe, and even in Mr Brower's extensive stock.

The cheerful Mr Brower, of the Cape Smythe Whaling and Trading Company, soon helped to reconcile Stefansson to the situation. After a day or two in his company, 'I was completely over the idea that the expedition was going to be uninteresting because of being too easy, or monotonous because of having someone to do everything for me.' Although it is three hundred miles north of the Arctic Circle, Cape Smythe had at that time three mails going to the outside world in winter. The first was due to leave by dog-sled in November, so Stefansson left at Cape

Smythe a report to the government at Ottawa to be carried out in the November mail.

He described its contents in his book:

I told the Minister of Naval Service that I considered it very doubtful whether the *Karluk* as a ship would survive the winter. I could not be sure in what part of the ocean she was, although inclined to the belief that she was to the westward. While the program of the expedition was necessarily curtailed, I did not consider that the lives of any of the crew were in danger, for if the ship were crushed during the winter the breaking would be so slow that they would have plenty of time to put off on the ice all stores and equipment necessary for a journey ashore. ... Regarding the prospects of the *Karluk* in general, I gave it as my opinion that she might or might not survive, but that the crew would be certain to get safely ashore if the wreck took place in winter, and would have a good chance of getting ashore even if it took place the coming summer. I mentioned that the eastern part of the north coast of Asia (Siberia) is well supplied with food, for it is a settled country with hospitable and well provisioned reindeer-herding or walrus-hunting natives and white traders scattered everywhere. If the *Karluk* were broken to the west of Barrow her crew had this hospitable coast for retreat.

He then went on to report the safe arrival of the *Alaska* and *Mary Sachs* at Collinson Point, conceding that the plan for the Southern Party would have to be abandoned meanwhile, since Collinson Point was more than 700 miles from their destination at Coronation Gulf. But he mapped out an alternative plan and announced that he was setting out immediately for Collinson Point to put it into operation. It involved redistribution of available supplies to compensate for the loss of the *Karluk's* cargo and to equip a small Stefansson party for a journey north over the ice.

He summed up his report as follows:

1. With the resources we had or could get we intended to do as much work this year as we could.
2. This year and the years following, whether the *Karluk* was lost or not, the expedition intended to try to carry on according to original plans, both in the Coronation Gulf and in the Beaufort Sea and Parry archipelago, where the main object was geographic discovery – the traversing and study of un-

explored seas, the discovery and mapping of unknown lands, and the further survey of islands already partly known.

Stefansson met with strong opposition from the Southern Party to the change in plan, particularly his intention to requisition some of the dwindling supplies for his northern trip. Eventually the Southern Party, under Dr Rudolph Anderson, set out on a long and arduous programme of scientific discovery which lasted until 1916, and Stefansson headed north on an ice trip which lasted five years.

Meanwhile his message to Ottawa set the telegraph wires humming all over the world. Canadian newspaper headlines screamed 'Karluk Missing', 'Stefansson's Lost Ship', '25 Men Missing in Arctic Ice'. The great Admiral Peary was interviewed about the *Karluk's* chances of survival. In Scotland Dr Bruce tried to reassure my poor mother, who every day read opinions and theories put forward by experts and lifted from the Canadian newspapers. Speculations as to whether we would be drowned in the Arctic or die trying to reach land across the floes were published side by side with lengthy dispatches from Stefansson describing his ice trip. At the start of a long report in the *Daily Chronicle* of 30 March 1914, he wrote: 'I am writing this in a trapper's cabin with a typewriter borrowed from the Royal North West Mounted Police post at Herschel Island. [At least somebody got there!] I am on a sledge trip making preparations for the survey of this delta in the spring, and I haul the typewriter along, writing when we stay anywhere awhile.' He added that just before sending the dispatch he had received news of the *Karluk* being seen to the north of Richard Island, and he proposed to set off at once and investigate the story.

But some newspaper reports were critical of Stefansson and his decision to continue with the expedition. He wrote in his book: 'The newspapers were saying that the entire complement of the *Karluk* had perished, that my plans were unsound, and that the expedition had failed. Editors especially, who presumably had been through high school, were asserting that all the knowledge ever gained in the Arctic was not worth the sacrifice of one young Canadian.'

Stefansson believed that the fighting of the Great War (which started, was fought and finished while he was on his northern trip) was worthwhile 'not so much to attain what was attained as to prevent what has been prevented. But I never could see how any one can extol the sacrifice of a million lives for political progress, who condemns the sacrifice of a dozen lives for scientific progress.'

I think there were few of us on the *Karluk* who would have disagreed with that sentiment, but as the ice pack swept us further and further away from our leader, we felt not so much like soldiers sacrificing ourselves to a great cause, as lambs left to the slaughter.

The Drift

As the gale increased in ferocity so our drift increased, and the danger of the ice splitting around the ship became so real that the Skipper gave orders that no one must go on to the ice without his permission. Everything that had been left on the ice – dogs, sledges, instruments – was brought aboard. Next day things quietened down slightly and we were able to move around again, but not for long. When we turned out on 26 September the gale was fiercer than ever, and drifting snow blotted out everything. Darkness added to our worries. We no longer had our long days without any night. The nights lengthened, and the sense of insecurity, aggravated by the storm, was intensified by the eeriness of the dark.

Still moving westward with the start of October we could see open water stretching tantalizingly all along to the south, little more than a hundred yards away, but we were firmly embedded in a floe which remained intact. There was not the slightest hope of our reaching that open water. Soon we were in the middle of a raging blizzard, and our ice floe, which had been stationary the previous day, was off again, WNW., averaging about sixteen knots. This led to a closing-up of all the leads, and our moving icefield began to meet with opposition. When adjoining floes raced together, the weaker floe would be pounded into pieces sometimes as large as a house, which would pile one on top of the other into huge ridges, then collapse and roll about as if they were as light as feathers; or one large floe would crack, the crack would open a few yards, the two pieces would come together again, one would be pushed under the other, and the upper one would be heaved higher and higher until, as it neared the vertical position, large chunks would break off and roll, rumbling and tumbling amid the crashing devastation.

The noise was deafening: thunderous rumbles far away, then not so distant, then nearer still; coming from all directions; rending, crashing, tearing noises; grating, screeching; toning down to drumming, booming, murmuring, gurgling, twanging – all the sounds of a gigantic orchestra. If only I had been a musician. What a theme for a great symphony! I might have out-Wagnered Wagner.

Our westward-driving ice had met with another area of ice driven by the north-flowing Japanese current, and some of us stood on deck and watched as the areas of pressure to the east, the south and the west crept slowly but inexorably towards the ship. I had no feeling of fear, only of awe and wonder at the gigantic forces that were at work, with a fleeting thought, perhaps, about what would happen if the area reached the ship. There was not much doubt about the outcome. All preparations had been made for a hasty retreat, but one could not help feeling that these were at best merely a token gesture.

Our drive eastward and finally northward, saved us for the time being at least. The pressure area did not reach us, the ice slackened, and, as if by a miracle, we found ourselves still embedded in the middle of a huge floe, two or three square miles in extent, with open water in every direction, but still not the remotest chance of freedom. We resumed our steady drift to the north and west. Then, unexpectedly for two days we were carried almost due east at rates which varied between five and twenty-six miles per day.

We were still confined to the ship, since cracks were developing and opening in the floe without warning, and we had to find ways to ward off boredom. The evenings were given over to chess and bridge. During the day a great deal of time was spent reading in our bunks, since there was not a single comfortable chair on board, except for those in Stefansson's cabin, which was now shared by Captain Bartlett and Hadley. Our little Eskimo family seemed to live quite contentedly in their cramped quarters. The children were no bother at all. I cannot remember, through all our ordeals, ever hearing one of them cry.

On Sunday 5 October, as if in compensation for our harrowing experience of a few days before, we had a display of the aurora which eclipsed anything I had ever seen. About 6.30 pm a single streamer appeared in the southeast, stretching across the jet-black sky to the west, and this gradually developed until the sky was alive with similar streamers. Then a small patch of light shone out near the zenith, gradually growing until it was about the size of a full moon. Suddenly from its centre there unrolled a huge curtain extending right down to ice level, folding and unfolding with lightning rapidity. In seconds of time this was repeated until there were seven such curtains hanging in the sky, waving and dancing as if blown by a mighty wind. The colour scheme was remarkable. A large stretch of vivid blood-red hung in the west, slowly changing to salmon pink, then yellow and later to green, which was the predominating colour. These colours were in vertical bands which chased one another across the curtains in quick succession.

I started to make rough sketches of the different forms, but I had to give up, spellbound with the indescribable beauty of it all. Then all at once I became aware of something new and strange, a consciousness of a 'presence', a feeling that I was not alone. 'Feeling' is not the word to describe it; there was nothing of the senses in it at all, only an awareness. H.G. Wells wrote that at times in the night and in rare lonely moments, 'I experience a sort of communion of myself with something great that is not myself.' Perhaps I was sharing a similar experience; I don't know. It passed, and suddenly I realized that when I had stopped sketching I had failed to replace my hands in my heavy fur gloves; my hands were numb. When I went below I found them white to the knuckles, and it took a long time to thaw them out. The excruciating pain taught me a lesson I was never to forget.

The spirits of the company were remarkably high, considering the uncertainty of our future, and the danger we were in. Everyone tried to find something useful to do. I made a medicine chest for the doctor, which pleased him immensely. When the Skipper saw it he slapped me behind the shoulder blades – a familiar gesture of his – and said, 'There are some people who thought they could only teach school until they came on this trip.' For a time I'd had a notion that he thought an Arctic expedition was no place for a schoolmaster.

We were now north of latitude 72° and approaching the northern limit of previous exploration in this area. On 8 October the doctor presented a letter to the Skipper asking that in view of the gravity of the situation he should call the staff together and lay his plans before us. Whatever his own private assessment of affairs, the Captain put a brave face on things. He told Mackay he had not yet given up hope of being able to free the ship. If this failed he would make all necessary preparations for wintering in the pack. If any of us needed anything we had only to ask and if it was on the ship we would have it. He saw no useful purpose in calling a formal meeting since, in his opinion, there was nothing to discuss. His reply seemed to me convincing and encouraging, showing he was in complete control of the situation, and most of us accepted it without reservations; but not all. Ten days later the doctor presented another letter. This time the Skipper refused to accept it.

Of course we all had our niggling worries. If the Captain's hopes of freedom came to nothing then all the slipshod preparatory arrangements made at the different stages of our journey would begin to have their adverse effects. All the things which were to have been done 'when we reach Herschel Island' would not now happen. Many essential stores which belonged to the *Karluk* were still on one or other of the two schooners. Perhaps most worrying, we had only one seamstress to make and repair winter clothing for the whole ship's company – an impossible task.

From 8 to 10 October we drifted due north, but from then on, except for the last week of that month, we were being carried steadily westward with occasional slight northerly or southerly variations, depending on the direction and force of the winds. Until then our soundings had never shown any depth above 20 fathoms, but on the eighth we recorded 56 fathoms, and four hours later we failed to find bottom at 68 fathoms. Next day we made a sounding every two hours, and the depth increased from 72 fathoms, with a bottom of blue mud, up to 95 fathoms, when we found a pebbly bottom. We set up our Kelvin Sounding Machine, and by the tenth the depth had increased to over 550 fathoms, so that we had to mount our Lucas Automatic Sounding Machine, operated through a hole in the ice at the ship's stern. At 995 fathoms we got a sample of the bottom, which was brown mud and sand. Winding in the wire was strenuous exercise, and working in relays, each relay winding in 100 fathoms, took us half an hour. The following day we had 1215 fathoms, about a mile-and-a-half deep, with the same bottom sample.

To add a little excitement to the monotony of winding, we made a com-

38

petition of it. Mamen and Malloch's best hundred fathoms took two minutes, beating Murray and me by fifteen seconds. Then we took to gambling on the results. Mamen and I had a bet on whether the next reading would show more or less than 1200 fathoms. Everybody crowded round, eagerly watching the indicator working round through 1180, 1190, 1195. Mamen was on the point of admitting defeat when suddenly the jolt came, showing that bottom had been reached – at exactly 1200 fathoms! Gales occasionally interfered with the sounding routine, but the soundings we did manage to get hovered around the 1000 mark, until on 1 November we were down to 110 fathoms. Thereafter on only three occasions, in the neighbourhood of latitude 73°, did we register more than 40 fathoms. For the rest of our drift we never found any depth exceeding 30 fathoms.

Whatever was happening Murray never missed an opportunity of dredging the depths. We built a snowhouse around the hole in the ice which we kept open at the stern of the ship, and only the most severe blizzards interrupted Murray's work. When the dredge was not in the ocean he was busy examining, identifying and preserving his specimens. It was an immense programme, carried out in desperately uncomfortable and difficult conditions, in almost total darkness, when our lives were in imminent danger, and any day, any hour might be our last. Murray's dredging usually involved all the scientific staff, and in the great depths, even the whole ship's company. The large dredge consisted of a bag about two feet deep, made of cotton twine of two-and-a-half inch mesh, which was secured to a heavy rectangular iron frame, measuring three feet by two feet. The line by which it was lowered was fastened to the middle of one of the longer sides of the frame. This ensured that the frame would remain vertical, with the bag trailing behind it.

When we were in a hundred fathoms or less it needed only six of us to haul in the dredge, and Murray got many interesting specimens, quite different from anything he had been catching in the shallower waters along the Alaskan coast. We believed we were now in an area hitherto unexplored, at least by anyone engaged in a scientific survey. Once we had reached depths of a mile and more and were using two miles of line, with a heavy dredge at the end, we had no need of any other exercise to keep fit. A block was rigged above the hole in the ice, the line was passed through this; then, in a long, single file, we all put our shoulders to the rope and marched off over the ice for a distance of 130 yards. Here we tied the line to an ice hummock and returned to repeat the performance, over and over and over again. It was an extremely cold and unpleasant, even distressing job, for we had no sooner finished one stint than our mittens and clothing were soaking wet, and on our return journey to the ice-hole they rapidly froze, to be partially thawed out by the next soaking with icy water. As the dredge neared the surface for the first time, we all gathered round the hole, eager with anticipation to see the strange creatures drawn from the great depths, but the dredge emerged from the hole inverted, and, of course, empty, and we had to start the whole process all over again.

Murray and Mackay lowered the dredge again, but it was carried away, with the loss of 250 fathoms of line. Munro had a new dredge made. It was lowered the next evening and left down all night. Next day we lengthened our drag across the ice to 180 yards, and it took us nineteen pulls before we brought the dredge to the surface. It contained two specimens – a brittle starfish and a spherical creature unknown to Murray. The third attempt yielded one solitary starfish; the fourth brought another empty net. On the last day of October, in the middle of a howling gale, Murray lowered his dredge yet again, but the blizzard intensified to such an extent that it was quite impossible to raise the dredge that day, and by next day it was gone. It had been carried away in the night and we had been carried into shallower waters, so that was the end of our explorations in deep waters. But Murray never gave up. He continued to dredge in shallower waters right to the end.

Malloch and I were the only other members of the staff who had a programme of work. Malloch could not, of course, do anything in his own field of geology, but he took on the task of making the observations and calculations which determined our position. He never missed an opportunity when weather permitted, and his work enabled our drift to be charted – a really rewarding piece of work in that it tied up with the drift of De Long's *Jeannette* and Nansen's *Fram* and established that there is a continuous circumpolar drift of the ice from the north coast of Alaska to Franz Josef Land and Spitzbergen. I kept a regular meteorological log but magnetic work was a waste of time; not only did the exposure to the weather conditions make the hours of routine work unbearable, but the unceasing movement of the ice made it impossible to maintain the necessary steadiness of the instruments. It would have been an easy matter to fake the readings in order to show something for my presence, but I preferred to be honest and admit that it was impossible to obtain any reliable results. I could only hope that the future would provide the opportunity to do some useful work. Meantime I had to agree with De Long's conclusion: 'Magnetic observations of any value', he wrote in his diary, 'are impossible.'

Apart from all that, we were mere passengers on the *Karluk*, and we were constantly reminded of the fact by a few croakers among the crew, who regarded us as a useless lot, enjoying privileges to which we were not entitled. It was the fault of the haphazard way in which the crew had been recruited. I now had sufficient experience to know that they lacked nothing in seamanship, but some of them were completely unsuited in temperament and habits to the life we were now leading. Many of them lacked understanding or appreciation of what motivated members of the scientific staff in embarking on such a venture as ours. To them it was merely another voyage, but with a much enhanced rate of pay. I could not be sure that they had been fully aware when they signed on that they might be wintering in the north (far less stuck in a drifting ice pack) for the Order-in-Council governing the expedition had set out that, after establishing a base on Prince Patrick Island, 'the *Karluk* should, if feasible, be sent south for the winter'.

So the days passed, without any change in our surroundings. We ate, drank and slept, wondering about the purpose of it all. We had accomplished nothing of what we had hoped to achieve, and there seemed not the slightest prospect of our ever being able to accomplish anything. All that faced us was failure, and the mood of depression in some of the men worked against the kind of *camaraderie* that might have made life more bearable in such difficult circumstances.

For my own part, I seized every opportunity of going for a walk over the ice, although we were under orders not to go beyond easy reach of the ship unaccompanied. Mamen and the Skipper went for a ski run one day. They were only about a hundred yards from the ship when someone shouted, 'Good God, look at the water!' About fifty yards away the ice had cracked and was opening rapidly. The two skiers saw it just in time, and managed to get across before the lead became impassible. They were accompanied by Hadley's little dog, Molly. She failed to make the crossing, but turned up safely the next day over the new ice that covered the lead. On another occasion, only thirty yards from the ship, I stooped to pick up one of my mittens and fell face-down into a deep snowdrift. For a time I could not recover my footing; my struggles only buried me more deeply. When I finally managed to get to my feet my clothing was soaking and my unprotected hand was severely frost-bitten.

On 14 October the regular routine of watch and watch was ended. One man stood watch all night, another all day. A fortnight later the final arrangements were made for wintering in the pack. We cut our meals to two a day – breakfast at 9 am, dinner at 4.40 pm. About one o'clock we could have tea and hard tack, and at night, from nine to ten, we had the choice of tea, coffee or cocoa. At 6 pm the night watchman went on his rounds, looking after fires and lights and seeing that the fresh water tanks did not freeze. He also had to keep a watchful eye on ice conditions and be ready to report any unusual happenings. All lights except the watchman's lantern were out at midnight. He called the cook and the day watch at 6 am (there was now very little difference between night and day, since the sun was above the horizon for only a very short time, and we had almost twenty-four hours of darkness). The boilers were blown down, the water drawn off, the engine disconnected and dismantled, and all water blown out of the pipes. For the next month the engineers over-hauled the engines thoroughly, painted the boiler and the funnel, and put everything in the engine-room in tip-top condition, ready for use if we were ever able to move under steam again. The crew spent two days unshipping the rudder. It was a long, ticklish job because of the heavy crustation of ice, but when freed it was found to be in excellent condition.

The job was finished in the teeth of a north-easterly gale which de-veloped in the afternoon of 30 October. This played havoc with the sur-rounding ice, which cracked and pressed in all directions, and we had some strenuous work getting everything that was on the ice back on board. The only opening that caused us trouble was the one between the ship and the place where the dogs were tethered. It was not too wide for us to jump across, but the dogs refused to jump and we had to heave them across one by one. We worked so hard and so hurriedly in the pitch darkness that we were hardly conscious of the screeching blizzard. By the time we had finished, our clothes were saturated inside with sweat and outside with snowdrift. But it was exhilarating to be so active, and we glowed inside and out when we got aboard and into dry clothing, rounding off with mug after mug of steaming tea.

Two days later the blizzard was still raging and we were confined to the ship. Captain was chafing at the bit, because there was an important job which he wanted done without delay.

Captain Bartlett had selected an area of very old ice which he reckoned
was thick enough to withstand any but the most severe pressure, and he
planned to set up a large depot of supplies there, in case we had to abandon
the ship suddenly. It would also lighten the ship and help her to ride above
the floes if the ice began to break and push against us. On the sixth day
of the blizzard he could wait no longer and gave orders to get the job
under way.

We began with the sacks of coal on the poop deck, and followed with
Murray's drums of alcohol, each of which weighed several hundred-
weights. By the time the brief mid-day twilight had gone we had cleared
the deck. Next morning the weather was a little better, and with the ice-
cracks closed up, we were able to use the dogs to haul the sledges, making
our work much easier. We removed all the cases of biscuits from the ship's
waist, casks of beef, and all our timber. Six days later we had the following
miscellaneous collection on the old floe:

250 sacks coal	33 cases gasoline
5 drums alcohol	3 cases codsteaks
6 cases codfish	4 cases dried eggs
114 cases biscuit	5 casks beef
19 barrels molasses	9 sledges
2000 feet timber	3 coal stoves with piping
2 wood stoves	

The Captain estimated that the ship would be so much lighter that she
would, if free of the ice, rise between two and three feet in the water.
We spent several days, therefore, chopping up the ice which was frozen
to the hull all round, to free her and let her rise. And she did rise. Whether

it would help when the crunch came only the future would tell, but we all agreed it was worth the trial.

The stores we had put on the old floe had been dumped anywhere because of the weather, but we now set about restoring some order. We began building a house. The sacks of coal, biscuit cases, alcohol drums, the casks of beef and all the more solid materials were built up for walls. The timber was used for flooring and for roof rafters. Across the rafters we spread the spare set of ship's sails. The sides of the house were then banked up all round with snow, making a snug and comfortable dwelling, which would provide shelter in the not unlikely event of the ship being crushed. A few weeks later we built another house, about fifteen feet square, and seven feet high, with additional material from the ship, but we had to use snow blocks for part of the walls. Until we needed them these houses served a very useful purpose as hospitals for dogs injured in the never-ending fights.

The Captain was not very enamoured of the Nome type of sledge which we carried. He much preferred the one with which he had become familiar on all his trips with Peary. This was built to Peary's own design, based on his experience during eight attempts to reach the North Pole. Now the Captain was able to find suitable employment for John Hadley by putting him and Second Officer Barker to the job of making four Peary sledges. Each was thirteen feet overall, with runners each made of a single piece of hickory or ash three inches wide and one-and-a-half inches thick, bent up at each end by steaming, and shod the whole length with a steel shoe, like the tire of a wheel. The bow had a long, low rake, and the stern turned up, making steering with the upstanders true and easy. The filling-in pieces were of oak, fastened with sealskin lashings. The bed of the sledge was made of boards of soft wood, lashed to the filling-in pieces. In loading, the bulk of the weight was always put in the middle, leaving each end light. With its long rake fore and aft, the sledge could swing as on a pivot. When the driver got into a position where it was impossible to go ahead, he could back the sledge, or turn it round, or even go stern first, without lifting it. None of these moves was possible with the Nome sledge except by lifting it, which was difficult, if not impossible, without first unloading. Being fixed with lashings instead of bolts, the Peary sledge was very flexible and adapted to the rough going over sea-ice. When it landed in young ice, because of the turned up rear end, it could quickly and easily be dragged on to firm ice with a rope if the young ice looked like breaking.

Mamen wrote of the Peary sledges in his diary: 'I for my part think they are both too heavy and too frail, so I suppose we won't get any satisfaction from them if they are to be used on a sleigh trip. They are only good for being photographed, Mr Hadley says, and perhaps he is right.' But they were both wrong. I used both types of sledge very often and my experience amply justified the Skipper's preference.

The Captain was worried about the supply of fresh meat. Whenever there was a lead or crack, or even a small hole in the ice, the Eskimos were there in search of seals. The seal is the most dependable source of meat in the midst of the Arctic pack; the polar bear comes a close second. Not only do seals supply food for both men and dogs, but their skins can be used for many purposes.

Kuraluk and Kataktovik were indefatigable hunters, going far afield, often five miles or more from the ship, before finding water. Two or three seals a day was the average bag. On 6 November they got ten in a very wide lead where many more were seen far beyond their reach. A week later six more were added to our larder, and a young bear no more than six feet long. When the animals were skinned the meat was stored in a large natural ice-box which we had hewn out of a hummock alongside the ship. By the middle of December we had about fifty seals and that one bear. The absence of bears puzzled us, for with all these seals around we expected that bears would be on their trail. But only once did we have a little excitement from that quarter, and it happened to be my twenty-fifth birthday. That morning tracks of two bears that looked like mother and cub were spotted within fifty yards of the ship, not many hours old. Mamen and Anderson followed them for five miles before being stopped by a large expanse of young ice which they decided would not take their weight. On the return journey they came across the tracks of another much larger bear, and later in the afternoon more tracks were found only twenty yards beyond the ship's bow, but it was too dark to track them for any distance. The man on watch had neither seen nor heard any sign of the bear, and it was strange that the dogs tethered all round had given no warning. At any rate, I did not have the birthday present that the morning's excitement had led me to hope for.

When Stefansson left us he took with him twelve of our best dogs, those supplied by Scotty Allan of Nome. This reduction in the number of our dogs was bound to create serious transport difficulties if we had to abandon ship. Every remaining dog was that much more valuable, and great care was lavished on them. Our main difficulty was to keep them from killing one another. When they were tethered on deck they were too close together and fights were continually breaking out. And once a fight started it was often a fight to the death. So, if the ice was quiet and the weather not too wild we transferred the whole lot to the ice; when it showed signs of cracking or breaking up badly we brought them all back on deck, where they kept up a continuous howling day and night. It was better when we had built the houses on the old floe. There were still fights, but we were able to put the casualties in one house, and all the other dogs in the second, and when we still had trouble, we got the Eskimos to dig separate kennels out of a huge snowdrift close to the starboard side of the ship, and in these we isolated the hoodlums, the militants of canine society. We never did manage entirely to eliminate dog fights. As soon as a yelp, or a series of yelps, announced the start of a scrap, every dog on the loose would bear down on the scene. It was a free-for-all until one unfortunate would go down, and then every other dog concentrated on him. The outcome was at least a serious surgical case, at worst another dead dog. In one fight two brother bobtails fought shoulder to shoulder against the rest of the pack until both were fatally injured. After the first died his brother lay on deck, howling day and night until he too succumbed to his injuries.

The howling and barking of the dogs was the only break in the black, icy silence that surrounded us. As the days passed without hope of release, we turned more and more in on ourselves, ever more dependent on the warmth and comfort inside the ship, and increasingly aware of the imperfections and deficiencies of the *Karluk*. She may have been what is termed 'well-found' for her original role as a fishery tender; she may even have been reasonably fitted for whaling, having in view the fact that normally she would not winter in the north; but she was sadly lacking in many minor refinements which would have made life just a little more tolerable in our present predicament. The saloon table, for instance, was too small to let us all sit down at meals together. Second Officer Barker lengthened the table to accommodate us all, but then we were short of crockery. There were only nine bowls and seven mugs. I had my soup in a sugar basin, and the soup bowls had to be washed for use as tea cups. We had only eight stools and two hard chairs. Malloch had to sit on a box, and my seat was a canister of dynamite.

We had only one pressure lamp, which gave an excellent light in the saloon, until early in November when it became so dim we could barely see to play chess. The only other form of lighting was by hurricane lamp, which caused headaches and eye strain. I took on the job of trying to repair our gasoline hurricane lamp, and after a whole day's work I got it working satisfactorily; but after ten minutes it went out completely. I took it all apart again, boiled every component part to ensure perfect cleanliness, fitted new gauze, and at the end it worked, and continued to work. I inspected my lamp every day, treating it as something beyond price. To contemplate life without it was unthinkable, for we would have darkness all round the clock for a long time to come. There may have been more lamps somewhere in the expedition's stores, but they were not in *Karluk* – and there would be no Herschel Island for us.

We carried out a major alteration in our cabin, which had eight bunks. These had all been occupied until our hunters left us, but now we were only four. With the Skipper's approval we tore down the four upper bunks and made cupboards from them. We had a coal-burning stove set on the deck between the remaining bunks and this made us reasonably comfortable. But the Captain was anxious to have our stove fitted up in one of the houses on the floe, ready for emergency. In its place we had the engineers carry the piping from the saloon stove through our cabin, but when the really cold weather set in, snow drifted into the piping on the deck above and was trapped at the right-angle bend, keeping the floor of our cabin perpetually under water. Then, when the cabin door was opened a blast of cold air rushed in, causing condensation which made the walls damp. At night-time the condensation froze, and we slept in a miniature ice palace, crystals sparkling in the light, gleaming icicles hanging from the deck above, some several inches long. All along the outer side of my bunk was a sheet of ice which melted when I got into bed, so that during the night the upper part of my blanket was sodden while the bottom half was like a small ice floe. We invited Captain Bartlett to have a look one night and we got our coal stove back.

The Captain had another idea for combating the rigours of winter. He got the crew to chip the upper deck clear of ice and sweep it clean. Then a covering of snow blocks about two feet thick was spread all over it. The Eskimos were given the job of piling snow blocks, eighteen inches thick, all round the sides of the ship, up to the level of the snow. We were then living in a giant igloo, effectively insulated against the lower temperatures still to come. A runway was built from the main deck to the ice, which made our passage from the ship to the floe much easier; it was protected by walls of snow-blocks down each side. Every door which we did not regard as essential was closed up and insulated with snow blocks. Wind breaks were built on the outsides of all other doors and at the ends of all passages which had to be kept open.

Out on the ice we occasionally practised building the traditional all-snow igloo, towards the day when we might need one, but we hadn't a good enough instructor. Igloo building was largely a lost art among the western-Alaskan Eskimos. Only Kuraluk was capable of producing anything like the real article and it took him, as we found later, an inordinately long time to finish the job. Kataktovik was a clumsy amateur by comparison.

So the Arctic winter closed in on our icy prison, and when the weather ruled out a walk on the ice, I would run at the double round and round the ship, or if gales made it impossible to leave the ship at all, I would find the longest passage in the *Karluk* and walk and run up and down until I was exhausted. I felt like a prisoner exercising in the prison yard.

9

The Lessons of
Jeannette *and* Fram

We were at pains to devise every means of keeping boredom at bay. Even those who, like myself, had never played chess, soon acquired sufficient skill to make a game with any opponent; if the inequality was too great we resorted to handicapping. We ran a league championship in which everyone aft, except the skipper and second mate Barker, took part. The winner's prize was a box of fifty cigars intended as a present for the police at Herschel Island. We followed this up with a knock-out competition which carried us along until about Christmas time.

During our various outdoor exercises we were gradually and painfully learning the dangers of frostbite. My only serious mishap, apart from my stupid behaviour when watching the aurora, and the time I dropped my mitten in the snow, was when Murray and I were taking a sounding and both of us had our hands badly nipped. The awkward thing about frostbite is that you don't realize the danger until it is too late, because once the damage has been done the bitten part loses all feeling. The most vulnerable parts are hands, feet and face, and the best means of prevention is to wriggle fingers and toes frequently and crease the face in a grimace. If there is no feeling then it's time to do something about it. Frostbite can occur in less than a minute, but usually it takes longer. Our method of thawing out the affected parts was to rub them gently at first and then more vigorously. Then came the pain, excruciating pain, not unlike the most acute bout of toothache, enough to make us cry out. Experiments many years later established that the best treatment was very rapid thawing by immersion in hot water. A much mistaken idea is that rubbing with snow is effective. The most elementary knowledge of science is enough to appreciate that rubbing with snow at a very low temperature can *cause* frostbite, and I was amazed to read in Mamen's diary that he used this treatment on at least two occasions. My first experience of frostbite left my hands in a pitiful mess, and it was days before I could use them with any freedom. But I learned my lesson and never again suffered anything but very minor nips to ears or nose.

Auntie, our one and only seamstress, was working against the clock making winter boots for all on board, something only she was skilled enough to do. For the leg parts of these she used the leg skins of reindeer killed during the late fall or winter when the fur is in its best condition. These she cut into strips which were sewn together, with sinew for thread, to form leggings. The soles were made from the skin of the *ugruk* (bearded seal), cut in the shape of the foot, but an inch larger all round. Then Auntie would chew the toe and heel into a ribbed pattern to bring the outside inch at right angles to the sole, and she would sew this turned-up edge to the legging, making a comfortable and watertight boot, or *makluk*. Her needlework was superlative and the seams were completely watertight without any further treatment. In fact she would have been deeply insulted if anyone had tried to grease one of her boots with the idea of making it more watertight.

None of us could even have hoped to help Auntie with this work, which demands a skill acquired only through years and generations of experience, but it was out of the question to expect her to make fur clothing for the entire ship's company. So we had to do it ourselves. First we had to prepare the skin, which was hard and stiff and crackly, and had to be properly tanned before being cut and sewn. This was done by scraping with a metal tool to break the vellum and make the skin soft and pliable. Auntie was the only one with a proper scraper, and Second Engineer Williamson had to make some for the rest of us by sawing up a shotgun barrel into suitable lengths and getting the carpenter to fit them with wooden handles. We were so awkward at the job it took us days to prepare one skin. When it came to the cutting-out, Auntie would look us up and down with her practised eye, and after a few slashes with her arc-shaped knife, she would hand us the pieces to fit together and sew. And day after day it was stitch, stitch, stitch, reminding me of Thomas Hood's 'woman in unwomanly rags', although we had not yet reached the stage of 'poverty, hunger and dirt'; we were to come to that later.

Before we graduated to making fur clothes we had some practice with Jaeger blanketing, from which we made mittens, socks and shirts. We also made snow overalls from Burberry cloth. Then we progressed to sheepskin. Many of our attempts were failures, and it was just as well that we had plenty of materials to work on. In the end we managed to get together an outfit of sorts. Whether the garments would stand up to the hard wear and tear of Arctic travel we were going to find out before long.

The sight of me struggling with a sewing needle amused Captain Bartlett hugely. His reaction was always the same when he found me engaged in some activity which he considered incompatible with the dignity of a schoolmaster. He would give a hearty, throaty chuckle, slap me on the back and roar, 'This is better than teaching school, eh boy? Just think, you would never have known what a handy fellow you are if you hadn't come along!' There were the odd days when things weren't going so well with me and I felt like telling him to go to the devil. But I never did. It was good to see him so light-hearted when I knew the load of anxiety that lay on his shoulders. From the end of October we were faced with gales of up to 80 miles an hour and lasting several days. In the main our drift followed the wind which took us steadily towards the west. By the middle of November we had reached Latitude 73°, which was our farthest north. Then for a month we went south or southwest, but thereafter it was almost entirely westward. The rate of drift varied; ten miles a day was common; during a gale in November we drifted twenty-three miles to the north in one day. On 18 December a blizzard started which lasted six days, with winds from sixty to eighty miles an hour.

When the wind dropped so did the temperature, sometimes as low as 50° Fahrenheit of frost. There were many alarms. Very often the ice would crack, leads would open, then close up or freeze over. A leak developed in the ship and we had to pump daily, by hand, because the boilers had been blown down.

As our drift carried us farther and farther westward, our chart showed that we were rapidly approaching the line followed by De Long in 1879 when the *Jeannette* was caught and crushed in the ice. As time went on our interest in that story, with its disastrous ending, began to affect our thoughts, influence our attitudes and moods. Every time Malloch determined a new position De Long's chart was brought out and laid alongside

KARLUK DRIFT (4 months) •••••
JEANNETTE DRIFT (21 months) ••••••
FRAM DRIFT (3 years) △—△—△
DE LONG'S SLED & BOAT JOURNEY ••••
NANSEN'S SLED & BOAT JOURNEY ═══

C. Farewell

Julianehaab

GREENLAND

ICELAND

HUDSON BAY

CANADA

CONJECTURAL DRIFT OF JEANNETTE RELICS

FRAM'S HOMEWARD ROUTE

Spitzbergen

FRAM BROKE FREE

FRAM'S OUTWARD ROUTE

NANSEN HOME BY SHIP

Franz Josef Land

Novaya Zemlya

VOYAGE

NAMSEN'S FARTHEST NORTH

FRAM'S DRIFT

PEARY 1908

Victoria Island

Banks Island

Prince Patrick Island

Flaxman Land

Heschel Island

ALASKA

Pt. Barrow

Colville R.

KARLUK'S DRIFT

KARLUK CRUSHED

KARLUK

JEANNETTE

JEANNETTE'S DRIFT

WRANGEL ISLAND

Herald Island

East Cape

Bering Strait

St Lawrence

Anadyr Gulf

FRAM FROZEN IN

FRAM'S OUTWARD

New Siberian Islands

JEANNETTE CRUSHED

Bennet Island

Lena Delta

S I B E R I A

53

our own. Distances were measured and compared, positions plotted. Discussions went on and on. Were we heading for the same disaster? What could we do to prevent it? Should we leave the ship before it happonod?

I avoided these gatherings because they always ended up in an atmosphere of gloom and despondency. But when there were no jobs to be done, or the weather was too bad for exercise, I spent the time in my bunk, studying in detail the eight hundred-odd pages of the record of De Long's expedition, not in any mood of foreboding, but rather to learn what could be learned from the example of men whose plight had so closely matched our own so far – and in the probable future. The *Jeannette* had drifted with the pack for nineteen months before cracking up and being abandoned. The company took to whale boats and some of them drowned, some of them reached land-ice only to perish in the attempt to reach safety in Siberia. Twenty of the crew of thirty-three died along with De Long himself. Three years later articles belonging to the *Jeannette* were picked up on an ice floe on the south-west coast of Greenland, showing that the ice had drifted across the polar basin, a distance of several thousand miles. On this evidence, Fridtjof Nansen, in 1893 in his specially built *Fram*, made fast to an ice floe, drifted north for six months to 84° 4′ N., then left the ship and, with one companion, crossed the ice to the highest latitude then attained, 86° 14′ N. Meanwhile the rest of his crew, under Captain Sverdrup, rode the ice-pack in the tailor-built *Fram* for nearly three years, drifting as far north as 85° 5′ N. and emerging into the open sea on 13 August 1896, the day Nansen arrived in Norway from Siberia.

Comparing these experiences with our own, it seemed to me absolutely inconceivable that the poor old *Karluk* would stand up to the ravages of the ice as the magnificent *Fram* had done. Could we even last as long as the *Jeannette*? That, too, was highly unlikely. The *Jeannette*, although not built to rise on top of the ice like the *Fram*, had been much stronger than the *Karluk*, and much more time and care had been devoted to her outfitting. The most likely possibility was that the *Karluk* would be crushed by the ice in the kind of conditions in which the crew of the *Jeannette* had been shipwrecked; but it would happen to us much sooner.

I never discussed my reflections with anyone else, and I never allowed my study of the De Long and Nansen diaries to depress me. Snuggled up in my bunk on the *Karluk*, as she drifted helplessly in exactly the same situation as those brave men had faced so many years ago, I concentrated on learning lessons from the observations they had taken the time and trouble to record. From the things which appeared to me to have been done which should not have been done, and the things which had not been done which ought to have been done, I gained experience, in theory at least, which I was sure would stand me in good stead whatever happened. And I was right. The future was to prove that I had profited from my reading. Meanwhile I was content to leave the future in the sure hands of Captain Bartlett.

But others were far from content. It grieved me that my Scottish colleagues, Dr Mackay and James Murray, seemed to be so much at variance with the skipper. Mamen told me that Mackay, Murray and Beuchat were planning to leave the ship and make their own way ashore.

Mamen, a Norwegian, had been invited to join the plan to leave the ship, but he refused. No one asked me, probably because I had, on the occasion of the doctor's first letter to the skipper, made it clear that I was with the Captain all the way. Mackay, Murray and Beuchat sat far into the small hours, after everybody had turned in, criticizing and planning. What they discussed the rest of us could only guess, but the skipper in his adjoining cabin must have heard everything they said. It was not surprising that relations between him and Dr Mackay were strained, for the doctor was clearly the leading spirit in the plot. He and the skipper had never exchanged a word since Captain Bartlett had refused to accept the doctor's second letter. There was no further request for a meeting, but it was clear that the three were serious in their intention to leave the ship when they started to make man-harness for hauling sledges, the method of transport Murray and Mackay had used in the Antarctic.

The skipper was a very lonely man. Responsibility, not of his choosing, for the lives of us scientists, as well as his crew, and the Eskimos and their children, weighed heavily upon him. I never made any attempt to invade the privacy of his cabin, but sometimes he invited me along. The first time he called me in to collect something or other, I noticed on his table a copy of Dean Hole's *A Book About Roses*. As I picked it up he asked, 'Do you grow roses?' And then we sat, in the midst of limitless ice, with between 60 and 70° Fahrenheit of frost outside, in perpetual darkness, numberless miles from the nearest garden, talking about roses. What an uplift that talk was to both of us! We progressed from roses to gardening in general. Later he lent me a book by Winston Churchill. When I returned it we sat discussing the problems of the working class and high society. Although, like myself, he had a working-class origin, he had an intimate personal acquaintance with American upper-class circles. He had made many friends in the course of piloting wealthy Americans on Arctic hunting trips, and he moved freely in American high society. I think he enjoyed these interludes as much as I did. They took our minds off our present problems for brief spells, kept us from looking in on ourselves, reminded us that there was still a familiar world that we would return to if we just kept our heads and took things calmly.

I also derived great pleasure from observing all the phenomena which occur so frequently in polar regions, because of the atmospheric conditions; parahelia with circles of prismatic colours; mock suns and inverted arches; paraselene with mock moons; coronas, blood-red haloes; the variety was unending. One night when there was a full moon I went for a walk on the ice and stopped about a hundred yards from the ship. The larger hummocks of ice stood out in all their weird shapes and sizes, casting fantastic shadows in the moonlight. The winds had swept their tops clear of snow, exposing glare-ice, which glistened like giant emeralds. All over the pack, the smaller lumps of ice scintillated in dazzling brilliance, like diamonds scattered in all directions as far as the eye could see. The stars shone in a cloudless sky, dimmed by the resplendent moon. A faint auroral arch was criss-crossed by shimmering dancing streamers. As I turned round to face the ship, old *Karluk* seemed to be doing her best to outdo nature. Her deck covering of snow shimmered like tinsel. Every rope and spar was magnified by a fluffy coating of frosted rime. Once again I became aware of what I can only describe as a Presence, which filled me with an exaltation beyond all earthly feeling. As it passed, and I walked back to the ship, I felt wholly convinced that no agnostic, no sceptic, no atheist, no humanist, no doubter, would ever take from me the certainty of the existence of God. Whatever hardships the future might hold, whatever fate the North had in store for me, I felt supremely glad I had come.

My feeling of calm, even happy resignation, took me right through the week of continuous gales, which battered our ship from 18 December until 24 December, raging up to eighty miles an hour and blinding us with snowdrift. There seemed to be every prospect of a very white Christmas, and everything else was pushed into the background of our minds as we prepared for celebrating Christmas Day. Williamson and I had prepared a programme of sports which we hoped to carry out on the ice. On Christmas Eve, when the wind moderated to a fresh breeze, we laid out a course for flat and obstacle races, making areas for jumping, shot-putting, and so on. It was impossible to find completely level patches, so our stadium was far short of Olympic standards, but by dinner-time on Christmas Eve we had everything ready. The Christmas spirit was taking hold, and when the Captain produced a bottle of whisky for the boys for'ard, and another for our mess, there were loud cheers. Officially we carried no intoxicating liquor, but we had a case of whisky on board intended as a gift from Stefansson to the Royal North-West Mounted Police when we reached Herschel. There were many requests for the tots of the teetotallers – Captain, Malloch and myself. I put mine up to the cut of the cards, and Mate Sandy Anderson won. There was a lot of laughter and joking, and for the first time in ages everyone was really looking forward to the next day.

At 5.30 on Christmas morning, Williamson, Anderson and I got busy decorating the saloon. We dug out the stock of international flags and hung them from the deck above, draping them all round the walls. Then, with ribbon which Hadley had meant for trading with the Eskimos in Banks land, we dressed everything we could in red, white and blue. On a large piece of sail canvas we painted Christmas greetings and suspended it opposite the skipper's end of the table. Behind his chair we draped the Canadian ensign. The result looked really festive and the boys coming in for breakfast were pleasantly surprised.

After breakfast we held our sports. It was bitterly cold, and muffled up as we were, slithering about and crashing on the ice, there was more likelihood of bones than records being broken. But the hazards brought out hidden resources of skill and agility. There were many minor injuries, but nothing serious, and after a rest we assembled in the saloon to eat our Christmas dinner. I had typed copies of the menu, which everyone tucked away carefully afterwards as a souvenir. Here it is:

DCS *Karluk*
Arctic Ocean
Lat. 72° 3′ 43″ N.; Long. 172° 48′ W.
Christmas Day, 1913

58

Dinner Menu
'Such a bustle ensued'
Mixed Pickles   Sweet Pickles
Oyster Soup
Lobster
Bear Steaks
Ox Tongue
Potatoes   Green Peas
Asparagus and Cream Sauce
Mince Pies   Plum Pudding
Mixed Nuts
Tea   Cake
Strawberries

'God rest you, merry gentlemen.'
. . . .

When we were all seated Captain Bartlett produced another bottle of
whisky and passed it round. In his own, Malloch's and my glass, he
poured just a drop, whispering to us to follow his example. Then, 'Fellows', he said, 'I want you to drink one toast. Stand, please.' And as we
stood up and held our glasses high, he led us in the toast – 'To the loved
ones at home.' It was a solemn moment, and we were all very quiet for
a few moments. Our thoughts were thousands of miles away.

It was a splendid meal, and when it was over the Captain produced
one of the boxes of 'goodies' presented by the good ladies of Victoria
for Christmas and New Year – cake, shortbread, cigars and sweets. After
that we were fit for nothing but lying on our bunks for the rest of
the day. In the evening we sat around smoking and listening to the
gramophone. We felt we ought to be doing something festive, but the
euphoria had gone, we had all over-eaten, and one by one we crept off to
bed.

Next day, just after breakfast, a loud report was heard, and we ran
out to find a crack in the ice running the whole starboard length of the
ship, hard against and breaking through the gangway, and stretching
fifty yards beyond the bow. This was something we had been dread-
ing, for it meant that in the event of ice pressure taking place in this area,

the ship would be right in the middle of a pressure ridge, and would be squeezed as if by a pair of giant nut-crackers.

Preparations were speeded up for abandoning ship. In addition to all the miscellaneous stores already on the ice, all the sledging rations were prepared and laid ready on the deck: *pemmican* (the Arctic explorer's 'iron ration', a concentrate of dried meat, fat and other nutritious ingredients); Primus stoves; tea (in tablet form) sewn up in handy packages.

Since our drift was now taking us closer to land – Herald Island and Wrangel Island, the first of many islands that lie north of the Siberian coast – the likelihood of greater ice pressure increased, and our anxiety accordingly. Everyone who was not fully fitted-out with fur clothing – and that really meant everyone – got busy dressing skins again for making up into trousers and shirts.

December 27: Malloch reported land to the south. The mate went up to the crow's nest but could see nothing. From the deck I could see a long, low line of cloud, which suggested the presence of land, and it was highly probable that we would soon be sighting Herald or Wrangel Island, or both. Next day the horizon was slightly hazy and we kept imagining we could see land. One of our dogs, Nellie, relieved the tension by giving birth to eleven pups, two of which died, leaving six dogs and three bitches. We had a feeling that one day we might need them.

December 29: The horizon was perfectly defined in parts and just about mid-day when I went to read my instruments in the noon twilight, I was sure I saw land, but not very distinctly. Straining my eyes I could clearly see a peak rising well above the horizon. I shouted to the mate in the 'barrel' and he had seen it, too. While he reported to the Captain I called everybody on deck, but by the time they got there a haze had settled and no one could see anything. They all thought it was a trick and I came in for some abuse, but just before two o'clock I went on the bridge and there, bearing SSW. stood a well-marked peak, black against the fast diminishing twilight, plain for all to see. I got a cheer to make up for the rude remarks of earlier, and I just had time to make a quick sketch of the outline before darkness swallowed it up.

It appeared to be too large to be Herald Island, which, according to our Pilot Book, was only four miles long. If it was Wrangel Island then we were at least two or three degrees of longitude farther west than our observations showed. In that case the peak would be Berry Peak, in the centre of Wrangel Island, about 2,500 feet high.

Mackay, Murray and Beuchat began to discuss their chances of making for land at once, and waiting there for the coming of hunters later in the year. The Captain, I felt sure, would not stop them going, but I was certain he would warn them of the foolhardiness of such a move. Next day there was no sight of the land, then, just as it was becoming almost too dark, the southern horizon cleared, and part of the island stood out sharply. It was comforting to know that land was so close, even though its presence might help create the very conditions which could crush our ship. When I went for a walk with Chafe in the afternoon we found a crack in the ice about a foot wide. It ran parallel to the ship, fore and aft, for a long way, then turned off at right angles for about thirty yards and turned again parallel to the ship. Where it turned, in an area of young ice, there were many narrow cracks in all directions. As we turned to go back to the ship, the young ice began to give way under our weight and sank about seven inches. The trouble with young sea-ice is that, unlike fresh water ice, it has marvellous elasticity. It will bend to an astonishing degree without breaking, so that one is liable to get too far away from strong ice before breaking through. This time we managed to leap back on to the old ice and report the new cracks, which were probably due to the proximity of the island. If we got a north-easterly gale – and one was threatening – we could look out for trouble.

Abandon Ship!

On the last day of 1913 nothing very strenuous was being done; everybody was reserving his energy for the grand football match on New Year's Day. The engineers and I spent hours making a ball. The cover was of sealskin, sewn in sections in the regulation pattern, and this was stuffed with sponges. A few practice kicks passed it as a reasonably good substitute for the genuine article, except that it had little or no bounce.

The fact that it was Hogmanay did not seem to have registered with any but the Scots; everybody seemed to be affected by a more than usual lethargy. About 11.30 some of us put on the gramophone and started a sing-song. We even tried a spot of dancing, and by the time the Captain brought in a Ne'erday bottle of whisky, everyone was beginning to get in the right mood. At midnight 'sixteen bells' was struck and I paraded the deck, fore and aft, raising the devil with the dinner-gong. Then we all gathered in the saloon to toast the New Year (lime juice for the abstainers) and we appointed Munro and Murray to first-foot the Captain with the remains of the whisky and a box of candied fruit. Then, standing round the mess-table we made the Arctic ring with 'Auld Lang Syne', and as a finale, each Scot recited something from Rabbie Burns, which delighted even those who could not understand a word we said. We went to bed with thoughts of home and loved ones.

January first, 1914: Immediately after breakfast Munro, Breddy and I went out to mark off a football pitch. The only reasonably level patch was the stretch of young ice which had so nearly landed Chafe and me in the water. Now it was strong enough to bear us, though it was cut up with numerous cracks, and had bumps and hollows here and there. It was a six-a-side international match; Scotland (Mackay, Murray,

McKinlay, Munro and Sandy Anderson, with a bit of Canadian help from Malloch) versus an all-nations team of six young bloods. We could not take any liberties with the pitch; apart from the unevenness of the surface, the ice with its thin layer of frozen snow was extremely treacherous. Although Scotland was sadly outclassed and soundly beaten by eight goals to three, it was a hard enjoyable game. Injuries were numerous, but none too serious. The skipper's was probably most painful; acting as referee, and about to start the game off, he absent-mindedly put a whistle to his lips, and it immediately froze to his skin. The loss of skin was extremely painful, and he had to finish the game with signs and shouts.

We played our football match not a day too soon. On 2 January I was wakened about 4 am by a curious sound, like the strumming of a banjo, just outside my bunk on the port side. Raising myself on my elbow, I put my ear close to the ship's side. At times it was a distinctly musical note, then it became a discordant noise; then silence. When it struck louder than before and the door of our cabin shuddered, the explanation dawned on me. It was the ice crushing and raftering (forming pressure ridges) some distance away. I lay awake listening until about six o'clock, fascinated by the extreme delicacy of the note which such a fearsome condition of things could produce. When I got up about 8.30 the sounds were closer, but nothing could be seen in the darkness, not even at noon in the mid-day twilight. I prayed that it might not come any nearer.

On the following day there was a breeze from the north, which we knew would be forcing the ice down on the land. We had been almost stationary for a day or two, but now the dredge line showed that we were off to the west again. Still the noise continued, all through the night. At half past six I was wakened by a very definite change. It now sounded like the beating of a drum, and then like distant gunfire. It continued all day, at times becoming louder and more violent as if it were getting nearer.

It was at this time that I noticed a change in the behaviour of one of our seamen. When I was waiting at night to read my instruments I generally passed some time with the watchman while he was having coffee in the galley. We had a Brady and a Breddy in the crew, and Brady was the most interesting of companions during the night watch. He had a wonderful fund of stories, and I looked forward to the nights he was on duty. But now he began to act strangely. He never answered when I spoke;

yet when he went on his rounds I could hear him singing loudly and talking to himself and the dogs. Back in the galley he became deaf and dumb again. His mates told me he had been acting queerly for a few weeks. He spoke to no one, took no part in games or voluntary activities; he refused his monthly ration of tobacco, and at Christmas and New Year turned down all the extra delicacies, even his tots of whisky – the surest sign of mental instability, according to his drouthy friends. I learned later that this kind of behaviour can be brought on during the period of total darkness, though it was by no means certain that the darkness was the prime cause in this case. All we could do was ignore his strange behaviour and hope he would come out of it.

We began to notice signs of economizing at meals. Whether this was done on the Captain's orders or the cook's own initiative no one seemed to know, but our milk was now diluted until it assumed a pale blue colour; tea, coffee and cocoa diminished in strength. Our cook, Bob Templeman, had several weaknesses (drugs among them) and was even more scornful than his mates of 'them scientists'. The skipper was extremely tolerant of his shortcomings, even his chain-smoking. When he rolled a fresh cigarette he just spat out the butt of the old one without bothering where it landed, and the only time I saw the skipper really angry was when Bob poured him his mid-day coffee with a cigarette-end floating on top of the mug.

Every possible precaution had been taken to lessen the impact of the disaster which every one of us now knew to be inevitable. Everything was ready, except in one department, and that was one of the most vital – clothing. We had plenty of untanned skins, but despite all our efforts, no stock of completed garments. We were far from being properly equipped to survive in the frozen world that awaited us outside the *Karluk*. Desperately, almost all day and every day, as the twanging, drumming, ominous ice sounds got louder and nearer we sewed, sewed, sewed. ...

About 4.45 am on Saturday, 10 January, I was wakened by a harsh grating sound, and a severe shudder shook the whole ship. When I got on deck the Captain and Hadley were already there. We found that the crack along the starboard length of the ship had opened slightly. Ahead of the bow it was about eighteen inches wide, and the dredge-house at the stern had been split in two. The grating noises continued without interruption, but so far the pressure did not appear to be very severe; the action of the ice was more in the nature of a sheering motion. The ship seemed to be rising on the starboard side. The deck, which had been about two inches above the gangway, was now a few inches higher, and kept on rising until it was a foot higher. In the hope that the *Karluk* might be rising above the ice pressure Captain gave orders to lighten her by clearing the snow blocks from the deck. But in fact she was not rising. The rise to starboard was due to the fact that she was gradually listing to port, and this went on until she was heeled over between twenty and twenty-five degrees. Then the ice cracked all along the port side and the list was slightly reduced. Everything appeared to settle, the noises ceased and the ice seemed to be still. Danger appeared to be over for the time being.

Our frantic sewing was resumed. I was sitting on the edge of my bunk, working on a pair of sheepskin socks when, about 6.45 pm, the grinding, grating noise started up again, right alongside my bunk. I said to Mamen, 'This is it, boy. I guess I'll get my boots on.' On deck it was almost impossible to make out what was going on. It was black as pitch, with a stinging snowdrift swirling through the air, driven by a screaming fifty-mile wind. The skipper was standing near the door to the engine-room, but most of the company were still playing cards or chess round the mess-room table, or sewing. Captain Bartlett went down into the engine-room and found water pouring through a ten-foot gash on the port side, just a little forward of my bunk. The ice astern had broken or worn off, and a jagged piece on the port side had pierced the planking and timbers of the engine-room, ripping off all the pump fixtures and putting the pump out of action beyond all hope of repair.

The inrush of water was so great that even the fullest pumping capacity would have been powerless to cope with it. The *Karluk* was doomed, and Captain Bartlett gave the order to abandon ship.

The operation of abandoning the *Karluk* was carried out with remarkable calmness and efficiency. There was absolutely no panic. Weather conditions could hardly have been worse. In the impenetrable darkness and the blinding snowdrift it was difficult to see where we were putting our feet – in the ocean, on a stable ice-cake, or on a small piece of ice which would tilt and up-end so that we had to skip lively to avoid being thrown into the water. There was a wide open lane on the port side, where our camp had been prepared, and we had to heave everything to starboard, where the ice was less disturbed, then try to bridge the port lead with a sledge. We got all our emergency stores and equipment to safety, and many extra boxes of foodstuffs from the ship's stores. The doctor was the only casualty. He fell into the sea, right up to the neck, and it was sheer luck that he was seen and pulled out in time. We got him on board on the starboard side and into the Skipper's cabin, where we tore off every frozen or sodden stitch, and entirely reclothed him in a woollen outfit.

The two Eskimos had been sent to clear out the box houses on the old floe, light stoves and get everything ready for us to move in. There was a great deal of banter, and Captain was looking like his old self and congratulating everyone on the night's work. Shortly after midnight the ensign was hoisted, then run-down again and hoisted for the last time, to remain flying until the end. At half-past two next morning when the houses were ready everyone was ordered to turn in. Sleep was beyond me, and I spent the early hours drying out my clothing, which was thoroughly soaked, inside with sweat, outside with water and snow.

The Captain alone remained on board the *Karluk*, but we paid him many a visit through the night. He had a huge fire roaring in the galley stove, and he had moved the gramophone in with the full stock of records. He played them one by one, throwing each record as it ended into the galley fire. He found Chopin's Funeral March, played it over and laid it aside. He was really very comfortable, eating when he felt like it and drinking plenty of coffee and tea. There was just enough ice pressure to keep the ship from sinking. The list to port caused the port side of the deck to be under water, but the skipper was high and dry in the galley and could walk along the deck on the starboard side to check for any change in the ice and keep an eye on the water level in the engine-room. He was careful always to keep clear a line of rapid retreat.

Meanwhile we were having a beanfeast in our houses on the ice. Rummaging among the boxes, we broke out a tin of ox tongue, tins of roast beef and mutton, several tins of salmon, tins of condensed milk, salt pork, cheese, and about half-a-dozen old loaves. Using a chopper as bread knife, tin-opener and cheese-cutter, we were able to enjoy a remarkably varied menu. We finished up with cigars.

All day the Captain remained on board. For hours nothing changed. The ship was full of water and only prevented from sinking by the grip of the ice. The ensign fluttered in a strong breeze blowing from WSW. About 3 pm the mate took a sounding with the hand lead, but found no bottom at 33 fathoms. Another try, with the Kelvin machine this time, found bottom at 38 fathoms. The temperature I found to be quite high, −17° Fahrenheit, 49 degrees of frost.

Then, at 3.15 a shout, 'She's going!' brought everyone on to the ice. The *Karluk* was settling down at the bow. As the minutes went by, the deck sank almost entirely under water. Captain Bartlett put the Funeral March on the Victrola. With the water running along the starboard side of the deck and pouring down the hatches, he waited at the rail until it came down level with the ice. Then he stepped off. The *Karluk* slowly settled by the bow and sank gradually, with a grating sound, until she was brought up by the bowsprit meeting the ice. A slight puff of steam marked the mounting of the water over the galley fire. Almost gracefully she continued downwards, not even the yards checking her course, until the foremast was immersed as high as the crow's nest. Then she seemed to straighten up, the head remaining stationary while the mainmast sank lower and lower, and finally, on an even keel, she was lost to view. The Canadian Blue Ensign fluttered until it cut through the water.

Captain Bartlett, deeply moved, stood right alongside her till she was gone. Not one of us but felt a wrench as the waters closed over the old ship. She had been a good sea-boat, but she had proved quite unsuited for her present job, cracking under ice pressure which by no stretch of imagination could be described as severe.

So there we were, on 11 January 1914, perched on an ice floe in the Arctic Ocean, twenty-two men, one woman, two children, sixteen dogs and a cat. Our position at the last reading, on 9 January, had been latitude 72° 12′ 48″ N., longitude 174° 59′ 15″ W. Now we were able to reap the benefits of the Captain's foresight. We had two substantial and comfortable houses on which we could rely for shelter for a long time. The sun was not due to show up for some time yet, and we had to look forward to a period of waiting until there would be enough light for travelling. There was nothing to be gained by setting out at a time when we could travel for only the few hours of dim twilight in the middle of the day.

Only the Captain, Hadley, and Kuraluk had any experience of Arctic ice travel. Mackay and Murray had never had to travel over sea ice during their stay in the Antarctic. The rest of us were wholly inexperienced, though we were well aware, from the accounts of the *Jeannette* and the *Fram*, of what was in front of us. With the possible exception of the doctor and his friends, everybody seemed to be perfectly content to spend some time in what were really comfortable and relatively safe quarters.

Our snow house was fifteen feet long and twelve feet wide, with wooden rafters and a canvas roof. As time went on we had some trouble with the melting of the snow walls, but we managed to keep them in good repair as long as the house was needed. The box-house was twenty-five feet long by eighteen feet wide, well banked up all round with snow. The boxes had been placed so that the tops faced inwards, making it possible to withdraw the contents and leave the empty cases as a cupboard. Of course all the boxes were of different shapes and sizes, making it difficult to achieve airtight walls. Peary thought of this when he was preparing for his last North Pole expedition, and insisted that every box was of uniform depth and width, the length varying according to the specific gravity of the contents. In this way every box fitted snugly, just like standard brick or stone. Still, we made the best of what we had, and with one end of the box house partitioned off as a kitchen, complete with a big cooking stove, we had a fairly snug little camp, which we christened Shipwreck Camp.

Everyone was in wonderfully high spirits, even Seaman Brady. On the night of the wreck, when things began to get lively, Brady began to behave like a normal human being. As time went on he became the life and soul of the party. So it looked as though it had not been the darkness that had got him down, but the monotony and boredom of life, the inactivity and the helplessness of our situation in the drifting ship. There was plenty to do now. Our first task was to make an inventory of all our supplies and arrange them in some kind of order. A large tent was pitched to serve as a storehouse for everything that was likely to suffer from exposure. The Captain put me in charge of all stores, and issued an order that only he or I was to enter the store. Here is what it contained:

70 suits underwear	2 large sacks skin boots
200 pairs Jaeger socks	(100 pairs)
6 fleece suits	100 pairs Jaeger mitts
100 fawn skins	6 Jaeger sweaters
20 deerskins	4 Burberry hunting suits
36 woollen shirts	12 sealskins
3 rolls Burberry gaber-	6 heavy winter skins
dine	2 large sacks deer legs
30 Jaeger caps	2 ugruk skins
2 rolls Jaeger blanketing	20 mattresses
	50 Jaeger blankets

On the floe outside, ready for quick loading:

4,056 pounds Underwood	matches
Pemican	2 boxes tea
5,222 pounds Hudson's Bay	2 boxes butter
Pemican	200 tins milk
3 drums coal oil	250 pounds sugar
15 cases coal oil	1 box cocoa
candles	2 boxes chocolate

Besides these supplies in the tent and on the floe, we had the coal, clothing and equipment which we had placed on the ice during the previous months. As well as ammunition and more supplies of pemmican, milk, clothing, tea, coffee, butter and sugar, this lot consisted of:

250 sacks coal	5 barrels beef
33 cases gasoline	2,000 feet timber
1 case codfish	1 extra suit sails
3 large cases codsteaks	9 sledges
4 cases dried eggs	3 coal stoves
5 drums alcohol	90 feet stove piping
14 cases Pilot bread	2 canoes

We still had plenty of seal meat, as well as beef, pork, bacon, egg powder, soup powder, tea, coffee, cocoa, butter and condensed milk. All the guns, rifles and ammunition were safely stored, apart from one box of shotgun ammunition. We searched for it repeatedly, but never found it, and there came a day when we bitterly regretted its loss. But that apart, we certainly had an impressive list of supplies. The only thing was that we would have to leave most of them behind when we started travelling. Time and the weather would decide how much we could take with us and how often we could return for supplies before our floe broke up or drifted away for ever.

Meanwhile it meant that we could eat pretty well what we wanted. The meals were plentiful and varied, though for some strange reason the cook insisted on serving miserably watery soup, which he said was nourishing because it had ham bones in it. We had plenty of soup powder to make a really strong soup, but Bob kept on using his collection of ham bones, under the impression that they added something to the water. After he had used them for about the ninth time I purloined them one night and dumped them in a hole in the ice!

One problem was fuel. It was dependent on several imponderables: whether driftwood might be found on Wrangel Island; whether we would be travelling as one large party, or in small groups; whether one small party would try to get to Siberia leaving the main group to wait for rescue. While Captain Bartlett studied these alternatives he got Mamen and me to test the Primus stoves and estimate the probable rate of oil consumption. We had ten stoves, two of a Swedish pattern and eight American ones. The two Swedish stoves worked perfectly and we kept them going to heat up the tent. Only five of the American stoves were satisfactory, giving us seven serviceable stoves in all. We determined how many fillings could be got from a gallon of fuel, measured how long a full stove burned, and how long it took to melt ice and boil water for tea for a party of four, reckoning three mugfulls per man. We found that a stove full of oil burned for five to six hours. Melting ice and boiling water for one meal took half an hour, so that one stoveful should cook eight to ten meals. A gallon filled a stove three and a half times, so a gallon should provide for twenty-eight meals, which at two meals a day would be sufficient for fourteen days. Making allowance for loss and spillage, we decided, with the Captain's approval, to allocate oil on the basis of a gallon of oil for eight days, which seemed to provide a sufficient safety margin. I managed to repair two of the rejected stoves and made canvas covers to protect the burners. The only worry was that there were not enough prickers for clearing the burners if they became choked. And nothing could replace them; nothing else served the purpose.

On 25 January the sun's upper rim just tipped the horizon after its long absence, so we had something else to celebrate besides Rabbie Burns's birthday. We had a feast, followed by a riotous evening of singing and dancing. We had found a case of oysters and the whole dinner was based on oysters in a wonderful variety of dishes. Outside it was a beautiful starry night, almost calm, with the thermometer registering well over seventy degrees of frost. But in the box house, with a well-stocked stove, we made the night warm with songs and choruses of then and long ago. We had other musical evenings in the box house, but we never quite reached the peak of Sunday, 25 January 1914, when Rabbie Burns was celebrated on an Arctic floe, with oysters instead of haggis.

Yet we were not a full party that night. Four days earlier four men had set out across the ice to establish our first shore camp on Wrangel Island. We would not have been so light-hearted on Burns Night if we had known that we would never see them again.

The Tragedy of the Mate's Party

Captain Bartlett had at first considered moving the whole party to Siberia, six sledges with four men (or two men, one woman and two children in one case), and four dogs to each sledge, man-hauling when necessary. After reaching the Siberian mainland by the shortest possible route from Wrangel Island, we would skirt the coast to North Cape and continue following the shore to St Lawrence Bay, or else cut down Kolutchin Bay to the same destination. If we came across any native settlements on the way, the majority would remain there while a small party forged ahead to the nearest point of contact with the Canadian authorities.

The Captain's second plan was to send a party of four men, with three sledges, each with a team of six dogs and loads of 400 pounds, to land on Wrangel Island. Mamen was to be in command, and, with the two Eskimos, he was to land the four men on the island with all the supplies and one sledge. Then Mamen and the Eskimos would return to Shipwreck Camp with the two sledges and all the dogs, carrying only the minimum supplies necessary for their return. The four men in the shore party would be First Officer Anderson, Second Officer Barker and Seamen Brady and King.

While this operation was in progress, the Captain proposed to send out small parties of two and three, with small loads to be cached at various points along the advance party's trail. Some of these caches might be lost in moving ice, but we had plenty to spare; some might survive, and the operation of caching would give us gradual experience of ice travel. When Mamen returned he would make a second journey, and land another party of four with similar loads, while the rest of us would continue with the short trips until there was longer daylight for extended travel.

The plan seemed a good one and Captain Bartlett settled for it. I had the loads made up; the Captain and Sandy checked them. A fierce south-westerly gale held them up for one day, but they got away on 21 January.

Mamen's written instructions from the Captain were as follows:

Dear Mamen,

You will leave tomorrow morning at 8 am for Wrangel Island with six men, eighteen dogs and three sledges loaded with Pemmican, Biscuits, Oil and personal outfit. Land, if possible, on Berry Point, leaving Mr Anderson, three men and one sledge. You taking back with you to camp enough supplies to last for return trip.

Should you fail to connect with us at the camp and when, after a reasonable time has been spent in trying to locate the trail, you will return to Wrangel Island and wait our arrival.

Yours sincerely,
R.A. Bartlett

The Mate's letter read:

My Dear Mr Anderson,

You will leave tomorrow morning with Mamen, three sledges, eighteen dogs, Mr Barker, Sailors King and Brady and the two Eskimos. The sledges are loaded with pemmican, biscuit and oil. You will find list of articles attached to this. When you reach Berry Point, Wrangel Island, you will be in charge of supplies. Kindly pay special attention to the uses of these. The rations are: 1 lb pemmican, 1 lb biscuit and tea per day. One gallon of oil will last you 10 days. Mamen will leave one sledge and the tent, taking back with him enough supplies to carry him to Shipwreck. Whilst on the island, you will endeavour to find game. Be sure and bring it to your camp. Also collect all the driftwood you can find.

Yours sincerely,
R.A. Bartlett

Once they reached land ice as distinct from drift ice, supplies would be unloaded and left for the shore party to sledge at their convenience. Should they at any point be held up by open water, they were to discharge supplies and return to camp, taking the risk of the supplies being lost. Since these were additional to the fifty days' rations to be carried on the final trip, their loss could easily be replaced from our very abundant stocks in camp.

They left us at 8.30 am, escorted for a short distance by some of the others. What happened after that was reported by Mamen when he returned, and recorded in his diary. They soon ran into some very rough ice and heavy snowdrifts, making the going very bad for both men and dogs. 'But', wrote Mamen 'we were forced to continue. All are relying on me for a happy result, and if I fail now, it will mean a great loss to the members of the expedition.' They spent sixteen hours in their snow-house that night, without a stove lit, with a storm raging which tore away their roof three times.

Next day: 'O, what a road we have! It is more than difficult and will take longer time than expected. . . . I have got both feet frozen; the left one was the worst. I was up twice but only after having rubbed them well with snow. I got the circulation back, and not enough that my feet were frozen, my nose was frozen too and my middle finger was badly frozen.'

Their next stage was eleven miles: 'We are all in good spirits and have a bright look on things. With a little luck, I hope that we will reach Wrangel Island tomorrow.' They had not yet had a sight of the land because of bad weather conditions.

Then came serious trouble. They had come to a wide lead: 'After hav-ing got the dogs unharnessed and thrown across, we had to drag the sledges ourselves. I was on the other side, helping with the sledges and the dogs when a wild fight started, and when I tried to separate the fighters I got my right knee hurt, I am not yet sure what it is. It is either the knee-cap or the ligament that is hurt. . . .' Distance travelled that day was nine miles.

Mamen's leg was no better next day and they had to redistribute their loads so that he could ride on a sledge. For the first time they saw the land to the southwest of their camp: 'We come closer and closer to the island; it is now quite distinct. The mountains rise sombrely and we can also see the lowland to the west dimly. I hope that we may reach the island tomorrow; it will be a joy to us and to the others.'

Then King got his right foot badly frozen: 'He rubbed it well with snow, but it did not help and it was only after he had his foot on Brady's stomach for an hour that it began to improve. . . .'

Next day: 'The land was southwest to south. The temperature was now more than 40 below zero. I was lashed to the sledge today too. The nights are unpleasant now. Everything in the way of clothing is soaking wet; the woollen blankets are awful; they look like dish rags. Distance travelled about nine niles in a straight line. ....'

January 27: 'The distance from the camp to the island is, I should think, considerably larger than we supposed. Beastly cold. ... We only got 8 miles closer to the island today.'

The following day: 'I don't think the boys can manage it much longer and then they also have considerable trouble with me. Had I only known how far it was to the island when I hurt my leg, I surely believe that I would have gone back. ... Now when we are so close to the island we must continue. I must send the Eskimos back and remain on the island myself.'

They only travelled four miles that day, continually having to unload and cross openings in the ice. After crossing one which was eight-and-a-half feet wide they came to an even bigger opening and had to sit the rest of the day waiting for it to freeze over. Their Primus stove was out of commission, 'It won't burn and a tin of paraffin (5 galls) has run out.'

The next day, after covering twelve miles, Mamen wrote: 'I have come to the conclusion that it is not Wrangel Island. It is a shock to us and to all in the camp.'

There followed a dreadful night when the ice opened up right outside their house. The rest of the boys got out, loaded the sledge for a quick getaway, fixed up a shelter for Mamen, then spent the night walking up and down to keep warm. Next day there was a great deal of movement in the ice. On 31 January '... the ice opens up and is drifting away from the land, so we cannot do anything today'.

Then follows a most extraordinary entry in Mamen's diary. Although he had recorded his conclusion that it was not Wrangel Island they were approaching, Mamen wrote: 'I decided to make ready to go back to head-quarters'; and on the following day:

Kuraluk, Kataktovik and I are now on our way back. It was hard to say goodbye to my travelling companions. They will now have to manage by themselves and try to get to the island. I could not wait and help them as there was considerable open water between the camp and the coast, but the distance is not more than five miles at the most, so they can manage and get there alone, and there is more use for me as well as for the dogs in the main camp.

He took with him the following letter from Sandy Anderson to the skipper:

Ice Pan near Herald Island

Cap. R.A. Bartlett,Sunday, Feb., 1st, 1914

Dear Sir,

I don't know whether you will altogether approve of my action in sending the dogs back before actually landing but as there is a possibility of having to wait several days before the ice closes again, I thought it best under the circumstances to camp here for the present to endeavour when the opportunity occurs to do the remainder by hand, especially as you will be anxious about the returning party. I don't know if the identity of the island will naturally upset your plans, but I will proceed under original instructions as if it were Wrangel Island and await developments.

The prolonged journey with such a large party has of course made large inroads on our stores, and the loss of the Coal Oil is more serious still, but we will do the best we can.

Mamen is taking a list of the stores in our possession and also a detailed account of the journey, so I will refrain from giving one.

I regret to report that one of the dogs was killed last night, although we had very little trouble previously.

Hoping Mamen gets back quickly and safely, and all is well in camp.

I beg to remain,
Your obedient servant,
A. Anderson

That letter was characteristic of Sandy. No thought of himself or the danger ahead, only of carrying out his orders, however mistaken the interpretation of these orders might be. Sandy and Mamen had been given the same order – 'Go to Wrangel Island.' And Mamen was in command until they landed there. But according to his own record he had decided to go back, leaving the four men thirty-eight miles from their real objective. Herald Island, if they ever managed to land there, was absolutely devoid of resources, and they had no dogs to get them to Wrangel Island.

They were never seen again, four young men with no grand ideas about exploring the Arctic, or finding new land, just four sailors trying to follow orders. Sandy Anderson was not yet twenty-one.

We were desperately worried when Mamen returned with the Eskimos on 3 February and made his report. We had kept a beacon burning for five days to guide them to the camp, which we knew would be extremely difficult to locate in the midst of thousands upon thousands of square miles of moving ice. We had burned a whaleboat, about a ton of coal, several cases of gasolene, a case or two of engine oil and a cask of alcohol before they arrived. After Mamen had eaten and had his knee-cap put back in place he made his report. While we were listening Murray came in to say that he and Mackay and Beuchat intended leaving next morning. The Captain, desperately worried about Sandy's party, tried to dissuade Murray, but he said their minds were made up; so the Captain finally decided that they could go – if they signed an agreement absolving him of all responsibility for the venture. That done, he said he would outfit them for the journey, and if at any time they wanted to come back, they would be welcome; if they got into difficulties he would do his best to help them.

Seaman Morris asked the Captain's permission to join the party, and they left us on Thursday, 5 February at 8 am. Mamen and I went out to see them off. I had been up most of the night, making a copy of the chart and all the information from the Pilot book which might be of use to them. We gave them a batch of letters to mail when they reached civilization. I never saw them again.

Captain was so worried about the Mate's party that he decided to send Mamen and the Eskimos back to Herald Island. Three days later they left, preceded by Chafe and Clam, who were going on a caching trip. Munro, Maurer and I accompanied Mamen for about a mile and a half when we caught up with Clam and Chafe. Clam had fallen through the ice, so we took him back to Shipwreck Camp, and Munro went with Chafe. We were not long back in camp when we saw a sledge coming across the ice. It was Munro, bringing back Mamen, whose knee had given out again. Munro then set out again, with Clam, who had changed into dry clothes. These two were now going on the caching trip, leaving Chafe to go to Herald Island with the Eskimos.

The rest of us settled down to wait. I kept up my walking and running exercise. I sewed and sewed. I sawed up frozen seal carcasses for the cook, and that really wore my temper to shreds. The heat generated by the saw thawed the blubber and I became coated with it, hands, arms, face and all my clothing. To make matters worse I got soaked through sitting on a slab of frozen meat. I was wearing a pair of pants which shone like a mirror after a month's accumulation of blubber, coal dust and oil. Every fold in them was cracking, every seam rotting. In desperation I boiled a pan of water and did my best to have a sponge bath. The oily feeling remained, but with a complete new suit of woollen underwear, I felt cleaner than I had been for a long time.

Then on 16 February Auntie called that she could hear dogs barking and from our high ice-hummock lookout tower we saw Chafe and the two Eskimos coming across the ice. They were a sledge short. They had not been able to land on Herald Island because of open water. For two days they had been adrift on a small ice-cake in a lead about three miles wide. In their struggle with the ice one Nome sledge was smashed to pieces. One of the dogs got out of his harness and ran off. He was never seen again. How we were going to miss those two teams Stefansson had taken to go hunting.

They were sure that the island was Herald Island, because they distinctly saw Wrangel Island to the west. But there was no sign of the Mate's party, and Chafe presumed that they had tried to get to Wrangel Island as instructed.

All this time Captain Bartlett was keeping up his policy of sending us out on short caching trips, to get experience of ice travel and of spending the night on the trail. He hoped, too, that once we had landed on Wrangel Island, those supplies which we had been depositing at varying distances from camp could be picked up by sledge to supplement our emergency rations. Most of these trips taught us painful lessons; some almost ended in tragedy. Frostbite was not uncommon, as when Clam's ear was swollen to about twice its normal size. The worst hazards were from open water. Munro and Malloch went in up to their waists on one trip, losing all their supplies and just managing to save the sledge and dogs.

On a few occasions these parties met the doctor's party. It was obvious that they were in real difficulties. Man-hauling their full sledge-load was too much for them, and Chafe found they were resorting to 'relaying' –

dragging only half of their load at a time and returning for the rest, so that an advance of one mile meant a journey of three miles. One night they had left half their supplies on young ice; the ice had bent and the stores were ruined by water. When Chafe offered them some tins of pemmican they refused, but they did accept share of a seal which Kataktovik had shot the previous day. Morris had a poisoned hand, and Chafe found Beuchat in a pitiable condition. He had been left with half of the stores while Mackay, Murray and Morris relayed the other half. Both hands and both feet were badly frozen and he could not get his feet into his boots. He had given up all hope of living, and told Chafe that they had made a bad mistake in leaving. Chafe offered to take him back to Shipwreck Camp, but he refused.

When Chafe left them the little party was altering course for Wrangel Island. That was the last that was seen of them. On the way back Chafe found himself on their old trail, and it was littered with things they had discarded, mittens, shirts, makluks. Their sleeping bags had been soaking wet and it seemed they had been in the habit of going to bed, without even removing their boots, which probably accounted for Beuchat's condition.

Chafe's story cast a gloom throughout the camp. There was nothing we could do about the doctor's party. They wanted to go their own way. But the Captain was desperately anxious to find the Mate's party, and he now decided that the time had come for us to leave Shipwreck Camp. We would all leave for Wrangel Island as soon as possible.

We had only twenty-two dogs left, some of them not very useful. Captain Bartlett decided we would travel in parties of four, with five dogs to each sledge (the two remaining dogs were quite useless). Each of us was ordered to make a set of man-harness, so we could add our efforts to those of the dogs. We were wholly confined to our houses; the winter was at its worst, with extremely low temperatures, or gale force winds with falling or drifting snow.

When the weather at last let up we were able to finish our preparations, and by 18 February we were as ready as we were ever likely to be. Captain Bartlett addressed us before we left: take every care and everything would turn out fine; the first parties would make straight for Wrangel Island, picking up any caches they found on the trail; the last group would go to Herald Island and, if possible, one or two would land and make sure that the Mate's party was not there, before going on to Wrangel Island.

On Tuesday, 19 February the first two parties were ready to leave. The sledges were all loaded and the dogs harnessed. One or two of the boys were not very keen to leave our comfortable camp and pleaded bad weather as the cause; but the day was bright and clear, the only drawback was a strong wind with drifting snow. The first party to leave included Hadley, Williamson, Breddy and Maurer, who had the ship's cat in a bag round his neck; the second party included Munro, Malloch, Chafe and Clam. The rest of us – Captain, Mamen, Kataktovik, Kuraluk, Auntie, the children and myself – waited to close up camp before leaving. We wanted a reliable check on what was left, for we hoped that once we had all landed, we might be able to send back small parties for additional supplies.

It took us five days to get everything in order and safely under cover. Then Captain wrote a message, which he put in a copper tank, screwing the lid on tightly:

Shipwreck Camp, Feb, 24, 1914
Left Camp 10 a.m. Wrangel Island bearing SSW. magnetic 40 miles distant. We go with 3 sledges, 12 dogs and supplies for 60 days.
DGS [Dominion Government Ship] *Karluk*
[Signed] R.A. Bartlett, Wm. L. McKinlay,
Bjarne Mamen, Kataktovik.

We were being optimistic in putting the distance to Wrangel Island at forty miles. It turned out to be eighty miles, and involved travelling a trail of well over a hundred miles. Kuraluk and his family led off at 9 am. Little Mugpi travelled on her mother's back. Helen perched on top of the baggage. The children never seemed to be affected by the cold or any of the hardships which laid low strong white men. During the trials that were to come, even when things were at their worst, we all saw to it that they had plenty to eat, and what would have been a major disaster in any ordinary family (such as when their house split right through the middle as they slept) affected them no more than, say, the overflowing of the washing machine might upset a family in our modern civilization.

The Captain, Mamen, Kataktovik and I divided a load of 700 pounds between two sledges. Kataktovik had three dogs and 300 pounds; Captain had four dogs and 400 pounds. With man-harness I helped pull the Captain's sledge. Mamen, with his suspect knee, was no more than a passenger. We were away at 10 am, quickly passed Camp 1 and reached Camp 2 at 3 pm, but we could see no sign of Kuraluk, so we kept pushing on, hoping to catch up with him before stopping for the night. But darkness fell and we had to give up. It was too dark to try and cut snow blocks and we had to sleep in a light summer tent. It was the coldest night I had ever spent, and I remembered Dr Bruce's advice about how to avoid frostbite: 'Wriggle your fingers and toes and wrinkle your face. Give your ears an occasional rub.' I did my best, but we were lying very closely huddled together, and the Captain's sleepy voice growled, 'If you can't lie still, boy, get out.' I lay still for a while, but

I was so cold that I eventually did get out, and I tramped around in the snow, trying to induce some warmth in my limbs.

We set off again at 6.30 am in darkness. At Camp 4 we saw signs that the Eskimos had shot a bear. Then we came to a fairly smooth stretch of ice and Captain gave me a spell at driving the sledge while he went ahead picking up the trail. All went well until we got into some hummocky ice. The bow of the Peary sledge struck the edge of a hummock and over went the whole outfit, with the dogs in a terrible tangle. I stood there cursing and yelling at the snarling mob, and then I realized that the Skipper was rolling on the ice, helpless with laughter. 'Oh boy', he said, 'I thought I knew all the swear words, but you have sure taught me some new ones.' I had to laugh, too, because never before in my life had I used a swear word, not even a mild 'damn'. Schoolmaster McKinlay was certainly getting his education!

About 3.30 pm we caught up with Kuraluk near Camp 5, about 200 yards beyond the second cache, left by Chafe, which had contained fifteen gallons of oil. We found eighty-eight tins of Underwood pemmican and three cases of biscuits, but it looked as if a bear had mauled the oil tins and all the oil was gone. The Captain was very upset. He would not have minded losing the other items, anything but the precious oil. He decided to send me back to Shipwreck Camp with Kataktovik next day to replace the loss.

Kuraluk had already built himself a traditional all-snow igloo, and we set about following his example. The job took a long time, and it was doubtful if the result was worth the discomfort of standing around awaiting its completion. If Kuraluk had not been there we would have followed what became our usual routine, erecting four vertical walls of snow blocks, with tent poles as rafters, over which were spread our tents and sledge covers. Our regular routine when making camp was simple and speedy. The snow blocks for the first tier were cut from where our floor was going to be. After we had cut suitable ice for making our tea (sea-water ice, old enough for the salt to have been weathered away), one man remained within the house area and got busy preparing the meal, while two others built the house round him. The fourth man fed the dogs and then helped with the building.

When the house was ready everybody went inside. Our boots were care-

The author, William McKinlay (*right*), with
Diamond Jenness, a New Zealander and one of the
anthropologists on the *Karluk*'s fateful voyage.

Vilhjalmur Stefansson (*right*), leader of the expedition, with two of the scientists on the journey: biologist Fritz Johanssen (*left*) and anthropologist Henri Beuchat (*center*).

Dr. Rudolph M.
Anderson,
leader of the
Southern Party.

John J. O'Neill, the geologist of the expedition and
one of five Canadians
among the scientific crew

George Wilkins,
the expedition's
Australian
photographer.

The scientific staff of the *Karluk*, May 1913: *(from left)* Johanssen, Murray, Beuchat, Mackay, Mamen, Jenness, McKinlay, Stefansson, O'Neill, Anderson.

Alexander 'Sandy' Anderson (*above*), the ship's twenty-year-old first officer, and chief engineer John Munro (*left*), both from Scotland.

The armour-plated bow of the *Karluk*, which proved
powerless against the pressure of the Arctic ice.

Preparing for departure: the *Karluk* at anchor, loading expedition stores at the naval dockyard in Esquimalt, British Columbia, shortly before the ship left for the north on 18 June 1913.

One of the crucial influences on the thinking of the *Karluk* expedition team once the ship drifted west of the Bering Strait was an awareness of the fate of the *Jeannette*, which had sunk in ice in 1881. Most of its officers and crew had died attempting to return to safety, but a set of posthumously published journals of the ship's leader, Lieutenant Commander De Long, included a drift chart that must have sent a chill through the *Karluk* crew, so closely did it follow their own course. These illustrations are taken from those journals, which may have impelled the decision by Mackay, Murray and Beuchat to break away from the main *Karluk* party.

The *Karluk* viewed from aloft, showing her deck cargo of coal, as she was caught in the ice off Camden Bay, August 1913.

The Eskimo family who remained with the expedition throughout, and to whose skills the survivors largely owed their lives: Kuraluk (the father), his wife Kiruk and their two daughters, Helen and Mugpi, aged five and three.

Kiruk, who would soon become known as 'Auntie' to the crew, fishing in a tide crack *(above)* and stripping the blubber from the skin of an *ugruk*, or bearded seal *(below)*.

Cutting up the walrus caught by Kuraluk on 20 June 1914:
Chafe, Hadley, Williamson, Kuraluk, Mugpi and Helen
(backs to camera) (*above*). McKinlay (*left*) and Kuraluk fashion the frame of a kayak from driftwood. Despite their limited tools—a hatchet, a snow-knife, and a set of skinning
knives—the kayak was successfully launched and proved a
valuable asset (*below*).

'Clam' Williams, one of the seamen, at ordeal's end.

The author,
William McKinlay,
cleaning his mug
in preparation for a
meal of blood
soup.

fully placed where they could not be knocked about; they would be hard as iron in the morning and simply could not be put on if they had been knocked out of shape. We ate our half pound of pemmican, our ration of biscuit, and drank mugfuls of steaming hot tea. Sugar and milk were added to the pot while the tea was brewing. Our milk was in one pound tins, the daily ration for four men, and it was always frozen. So the tin was cut in two with a hatchet, one half of the contents dropped into the pot, the other half left for the morning. When it was being cut, chips of frozen milk were scattered around and someone discovered that they tasted like caramel toffees. Soon most of the men were chewing their milk ration and taking their tea without it. I resisted the temptation, and the day came when I was the only one left with a milk ration. And a real blessing it proved to be.

Having eaten we prepared for sleep. If our undershirt was damp we changed it. Our stockings were removed and dry ones pulled on. When we lay down we put our damp stockings across our chest to be dry by morning. The condensation from the roof fell on us during the night, so that by morning we were well covered with crystals, but generally speaking we fared not too uncomfortably.

That night in our all-snow igloo we slept very soundly, but during the night Kataktovik woke up saying he could hear the ice cracking. It had opened in front of Kuraluk's igloo and there was a widening lead a few yards behind ours. We came out to the familiar sounds of breaking ice, grinding and crushing and raftering. The darkness was impenetrable, and we had to be really agile to save ourselves and our outfit from being engulfed. It was while we were busy trying to transfer everything to a place of comparative safety that Kuraluk's igloo split clean through the middle, and in a few seconds there was a lane of water just where little Mugpi and Helen had been sleeping.

As soon as the light was good enough Kataktovik and I set off with a seven-dog team back over the forty-odd miles to Shipwreck Camp. We reached it about three o'clock, a good effort, because the ice was still cracking and raftering as we travelled, leads opening and closing, and we found that as we moved northwards, the trail had drifted considerably to the west. It was obvious that the north wind which had been blowing for a few days was responsible for all the commotion. The ice was being driven down on to the north coast of the island, and the pressure was being transmitted as far north as we were now, and probably much farther north. The old floe at Shipwreck Camp was still intact, though sadly broken at its outer edges.

We rustled up a wonderful meal, and loaded our sledges ready for the morning. We were on our way at first light, and for a time we made rapid progress. Then the going got worse and worse and finally we lost the trail altogether. But we spotted a flag that Captain had planted on a high hummock a little way from camp, and we were back by 3.30 pm to Captain's surprise and delight.

The supplies we had brought made our next day's load very heavy. Ordinarily I disliked a mid-day halt, for it meant standing around getting cold while the tea was made, but now the tea-break was a blessed relief. Tea was the only part of our meals that I enjoyed. I had taken an early dislike to our staple diet – pemmican; the Hudson's Bay variety was too fatty; the Underwood was too sweet. I depended on tea to wash it down.

Just as we were hitching up again we sighted the Munro and Hadley parties and we could hardly believe our eyes, because they were travelling north, back the way we had come. They told us they had been stopped by exceptionally rough ice and immense pressure ridges, rising to terrifying heights of up to a hundred feet. They had decided it was impossible to get through and were on their way back to Shipwreck Camp. The Skipper was speechless at first, and then he asked them just what they intended doing when they reached Shipwreck. Their rather sheepish replies showed they hadn't thought so far ahead, and he raged at them for their folly in risking the loss of all they had achieved up to that point.

Then he ordered them to fall into line, and with our party leading, we began to cut our way through the rough ice. After 300 yards we looked for a place to camp. It was impossible to find ice flat enough to accommodate a tent; building a snow-house was utterly out of the question. But we managed in the end to get our tents pitched somehow, separated from one another by large stretches of the roughest ice. The Captain went forward to reconnoitre, and found that the ice ridges stretched east and west, all along the north coast of Wrangel Island. It seemed impossible that we would ever get through that barrier of ice. It was a whole series of parallel ridges, rising up to a hundred feet, here and there perhaps higher, and extending in depth towards the land. At a conservative estimate the ridges covered a distance of three miles!

To make matters worse Malloch's feet were badly frostbitten, two toes and the heel on both feet. He had let them go without telling anyone and they were in very bad shape. Both of Maurer's feet were bitten. We could only hope that in the time we were going to take to get through the next obstacle their feet would heal. The idea of transporting invalids over the miles ahead was unthinkable. Captain asked me what I thought the chances were of another trip to Shipwreck Camp for additional supplies to tide us over the delay in getting through the ice barrier. Although the continuous drift of the ice and the breaking up of the trail diminished the chances of finding the camp, I thought it could be done, and he decided to send me with Hadley and Chafe to bring back as much as we could carry.

We left next morning with two sledges and fourteen dogs, and although different parts of the trail had drifted different distances, and the camp was almost completely obliterated by snow-drift, we had covered the fifty to sixty by three o'clock. We spent the next day drying our clothes and making up our loads – 800 pounds on each sledge. I made an addition to the message the Captain had left in the tank, giving the latest state of affairs. I wonder what happened to it, and the thousands of other articles left behind. Were they all devoured in the ice, or did they drift thousands of miles to be washed up on some Atlantic shore? We were saying a final farewell to Shipwreck Camp when we left next morning; this was the last successful trip to our friendly floe.

It took us almost five hours to reach the first camp with our heavy loads. At that rate it would have taken us a week to catch up, so I abandoned part of our load. The trail was badly smashed up and difficult to follow, and we had to pick and chop a way through many new ridges. I was busy cutting a path through one large ridge. Hadley and Chafe had gone to look for the trail on the other side. Suddenly the dogs began barking furiously. I turned round, and there was a polar bear, about fifteen yards away. He began to move round in an arc, keeping a constant distance from the dogs, which were harnessed to the sledge. I suppose I should have rushed for the rifle on the sledge, but it never entered my head. I stood only a few feet away, fascinated by the movements of this beautiful creature. My only previous acquaintance with polar bears had been at Edinburgh Zoo, and I had always loved to watch them moving around, swinging their massive heads. Now I had no thought of the danger from those huge paws. I just stood admiring the to-and-fro motion of his head, the dainty footfalls as he pirouetted around like a ballet dancer.

Then Hadley burst on the scene, grabbed the rifle, pulled the trigger. Click! The oil on the cartridge had frozen. He fired again and the bear fell to the ice. What a beauty he was!

We spent that night in a ready-made igloo, the one we had vacated the night Kuraluk's was split in two. I was feeding the dogs when they started barking, and I looked up to find another bear, a much bigger one, facing me across the sledge. I had only to stretch out my arm and I could have touched him on the nose. Again the rifle was on the sledge. Hadley made a leap for it, dropped to his knee and fired. The bear turned and was running away when Hadley fired again. Twenty yards away it took a leap into the air, turned a complete somersault and fell with a crash, which left a deep depression in the frozen snow and ice.

We thought that was more than enough excitement for one day, but just as we were about to turn in another bear appeared, and Hadley's first shot in the gathering darkness only wounded him. It was too dark to follow a wounded bear, but in the morning we followed the trail of blood and found him still breathing, but helpless. One shot finished him. We fed the dogs all the bear meat they could eat, and cut off a ham to carry along with us. I felt rather sad. I knew the bears were dangerous, and I also knew our lives might depend on being able to kill them. But they were such magnificent animals. I hoped we would never kill one except for self-protection or for food.

We had been away a week now, and I had an idea the Captain might be worrying about us. Sure enough, we met Munro and a party who had been sent back across three miles of raftered ice to look for us. It was the second time they had been out searching. Camp had been pushed forward three miles while we were away – three miles through ridge, after ridge, after ridge. To make a path the top edge of each ridge had to be broken down until the broken pieces were piled up against the vertical face, forming a slope up which a sledge could be dragged. When the sledge reached the top it had to be held poised until men could get to the other side and hold it back before it crashed down the other side.

The boys had done a marvellous job to get so far. Munro piloted us along the narrow path they had cut, and the roar of welcome that greeted us was only exceeded by the one that went up when we produced the bear meat. Next day some of us went back to collect the rest of the meat. Those bears must have been hungry when they called on us. When we cut up the carcasses all that the three stomachs contained was a collection of pebbles.

The Captain Goes for Help

We were still not through the pressure ridges; another four miles
did not see the end of them, but they were nothing compared with
what we had been through. Although we were still many miles from land,
we at last reached ice which could not possibly move until the summer
break-up. We had been lucky. If we had been earlier, when northerly
gales were forming the ridges, or if a strong southerly off-shore had set
all that ice careering northwards, we would have been finished. We had
just missed that fate by a few days.

But the doctor's party must have been right in the middle of that moun-
tainous sea of moving ice. Recently the National Archives in Ottawa sent
me a copy of correspondence between Stefansson and Second Engineer
Williamson in 1959. Williamson was recalling how his party had been
stopped by the barrier of ice ridges. That was at the point where we met
them on their way back to Shipwreck Camp, and Captain Bartlett ordered
them to turn round again. Williamson wrote: 'On nearing the ridge, we
espied a black flag waving on a stick and on approaching it over very
much rough ice, found that it was a sailor's scarf, which must have
belonged to Anderson's party, but no signs of them. What became of the
scarf I do not know.'

This was never reported to the Captain. If it had been we would have
been in no doubt about its significance. It was highly improbable that
the scarf belonged to anyone in the Mate's party; it was hardly likely
that it had drifted all the way from Herald Island. It was much more
likely that it belonged to Seaman Morris, who had gone with the doctor's
party, and it was a clear pointer to what had happened to them. The
night Kuraluk's igloo was split in two, when we had felt the terrifying

tail-end of the moving ice, Mackay, Murray, Beuchat and Morris must have been in the centre of those immense ridges as the gale piled them higher and higher against the immovable miles of land-locked ice. That area would be like some nightmare storm at sea, in which waves rising to a hundred feet and more would be made of solid ice, crashing and tumbling down in pieces as big as houses. There could be no hope for the doctor's party.

There were still a few smaller ridges through which we had to pick a way, and we were now hampered by snow which reached our thighs, making the going slow, laborious and painful. The sky was entirely covered with cloud, but not densely enough to prevent diffused sunlight, nor to produce shadows. The result was that the surface of the ice and snow appeared quite flat, with no shadows to warn of hummocks and snowdrifts into which we stumbled and fell time after time. These were ideal conditions for causing snow-blindness. We had two kinds of snow-goggles. Our amber-coloured glasses frosted up with condensation, making it impossible to see; we had to remove them repeatedly to clear them. The other type had metal eye-pieces with several slits in them; these were modelled on Eskimo goggles, which had wooden eye-pieces. The drawback with these was their extremely limited field of vision. We could see only a short distance beyond our feet, and we could not see to the side at all. But we dared not travel without goggles of one kind or another, particularly in this diffused light, which caused eye-strain, leading quickly to snow-blindness.

But these hazards were nothing to what we had been through in the battle with the ice ridges, and we progressed cheerfully at the rate of about ten miles a day. We were relaying our supplies in light loads, so that we were travelling sometimes twice, sometimes three times the distance we actually advanced, but we found this easier than dragging heavy loads. At last we reached really smooth ice and were within a few miles of land. We had a chance to relax and time to reflect on our situation. It was true we had lost our ship, but we had lost her at a season which was near the ideal for sea-ice travel. We'd had some stormy weather, but only on that one occasion when we were approaching the last pressure area had we ever been in extreme danger. We had successfully surmounted that obstacle, which Hadley said was

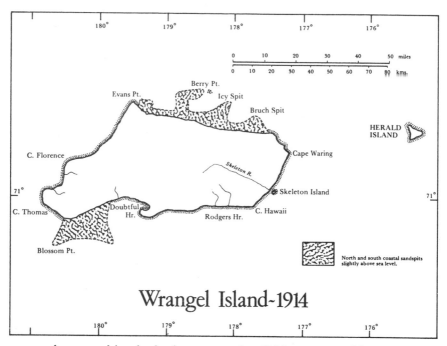

Wrangel Island~1914

worse than anything he had ever seen in all his twenty-odd years in the Arctic.

So we were in high spirits when we reached our most forward cache and Kataktovik took over the job of breaking trail. We had gone about seven miles further and the land seemed no nearer when Kataktovik scuffled the snow with his foot. Then he leaped into the air, waving his arms and shouting, 'Nuna! Nuna!' (Land!). Mamen and I gave a cheer which we hoped would carry to those coming up behind. We stood looking around the unbroken white expanse, with nothing but that little patch to show that our feet were truly on firm ground, the first since leaving Port Clarence eight months before. It was now 12 March 1914.

As we moved around we discovered a large amount of driftwood under the snow, and we heaved a sigh of relief. This would solve our fuel problem. All that remained now was to investigate game prospects. We were not quite sure on what part of the island we had landed, though it was certainly part of the long sandspit that stretched along the north coast, separated from the mainland by a wide lagoon. We identified it later as Icy Spit.

We built a shelter in our usual fashion of four vertical walls of snow blocks, roofed over with our tent and sledge covers. It was a makeshift affair and we spent an extremely cold night, but next day was one of beautiful sunshine, though the thermometer registered eighty degrees of frost. Apart from the need to keep moving, and to guard against frostbite, it was a perfect day that generated a spirit of real optimism. We were on land, and it was good to be alive.

We were able to dry out all our wet clothing and furs at a huge log fire. We made several trips over the last part of the trail to bring in the supplies left at different points, and by evening everything was safe in camp. As usual on a strenuous day we perspired freely and the fur on the inner side of our undershirts was soaking. Now, when there was no wind blowing, all we had to do was to strip to the waist, turn our undershirts inside out, fur outwards. In an instant the perspiration was frozen, and with a few flicks of a small stick, it was gone. Our shirts were perfectly dry, and we could put them on again immediately. The process was so quick that our naked torsos suffered no ill effects from the exposure.

Kuraluk had taken a long walk westward and found no trace of anyone having landed there. He saw no tracks of animals and he was not at all optimistic about our chances of game. He also thought we were unlikely to get seals, because the ice was firmly grounded for thirty miles northwards, and there would be no open water until the summer. Later he went across the lagoon towards the mountains and saw two fresh bear tracks, but he was emphatic that there were no caribou on the island.

Captain's original plan to lead us all to the Siberian mainland was no longer feasible. The physical condition of the majority of the party was so poor that to take them all on such a hazardous trip was inviting whole-sale disaster. So he decided that he would make the crossing himself, with Kataktovik, and try to reach civilization so that relief measures might be organized. He gave orders for Mamen, Chafe and Clam to return to Shipwreck Camp for more supplies. The Skipper would take seven dogs. Mamen would have the remainder and would bring as many loads as possible to the landward side of the ridges; from there they could be relayed at leisure over the grounded ice.

This decision was a great blow to Malloch and Mamen. Malloch had made no secret of the fact that he was anxious to go with the Captain, and he did all he could to persuade him to change his mind. When the Skipper refused, poor Malloch nearly went to pieces. Mamen reacted badly too. On Monday, 2 March, he had written in his diary that the Captain ordered him to stay in camp and rest his leg because 'you know that you will have use for it before you and I get through'. Mamen took this to mean, 'It will probably be the Captain, Kataktovik and I who will go over to Siberia for help.' When he heard that he was not being included in the party, Mamen wrote: 'The Captain begins to be queer now, it seems to me. When we came home tonight he said, "I don't give a damn now till we get the things in to the island then to hell with them, with everybody. I know damn well to look out for myself. ..." Yes, he looks out for himself, or rather, Cloud (Kataktovik) is his nursemaid. He must have help in everything; he cannot do a thing alone.'

Mamen's diary is in the National Archives in Ottawa and available to polar researchers. Though I am prepared to accept that the Skipper might have lost his temper at the attitude of some of the moaners in the party, I am sure he did not say, and certainly did not mean, that he would 'look out for himself'. It was wholly alien to his character. Everywhere else Mamen's diary is full of admiration and praise for the Skipper, and this outburst was just a measure of his deep disappointment at being left behind.

Chief Engineer Munro, the senior officer after Sandy Anderson, would be in command on the island. Captain was well aware of the strains and stresses that ran through the whole outfit. There was bad feeling between Mamen and Munro, dating back to the days on board ship, and Munro's relations with his shipmates, Williamson and Breddy, could scarcely be described as cordial. But there was nothing the Skipper could do about that. He arranged that we should be divided into four parties, each with its own allocation of supplies, and each free to settle where it pleased, subject to Munro's overall approval. The Captain's idea was that by being dispersed at intervals of from ten to fifteen miles, we would be able to cover a much larger area in hunting. Kuraluk and Hadley were to hunt for the whole party, as well as each group trying for its own game.

As it happened the weather broke, and while we were trying to repair our roof, which was sagging under the weight of several feet of snow,

Mamen put his knee-cap out again, and we had a good deal of trouble getting it fixed. This put paid to any last hope he might have had of going with the Captain. It also ruled him out of the trip back to Shipwreck Camp. Chafe and Williamson were sick. The cook was under the weather, so Munro decided to make the trip to Shipwreck with Breddy and Clam. Once they had left I turned my attention to the preparations for the Captain's departure. On his instructions I divided all the supplies in the camp and made a copy of the allocations, which I signed, for delivery to Ottawa. The allocation was made as follows:

Parties 1 and 2 (4 men each party)	Parties 3 and 4 (3 men each party)
222 lb Underwood pemmican	168 lb Underwood pemmican
96 lb Hudson's Bay pemmican	72 lb Hudson's Bay pemmican
1½ cases biscuits	1 case biscuits
10 gallons oil	10 gallons oil

With a ration of one pound of pemmican per man per day, there was enough for eighty days; but biscuits would not last as long. For the dogs there remained only 120 lb pemmican; it had evidently been used very extravagantly on the journey ashore.

To the Captain and Kataktovik I allocated: 96 lb Underwood pemmican, 192 lb dog pemmican, eight gallons of oil. Sugar and tea had already been issued, and all the milk (except my own ration) had been eaten as toffee on the trail.

I loaded up the Captain's sledge, and while we waited for travelling weather, Kuraluk and Kataktovik were busy building an all-snow igloo. When it was finished we dismantled our house so that the Captain could have his tent, which had formed part of our roof. After the Captain's departure, the new igloo was to be occupied by Hadley, with Kuraluk and his family. Mamen, Malloch, Templeman and I moved into Kuraluk's old house. The night before the Captain's departure I sat up late making lists and writing letters for him to post when he reached civilization.

In *Last Voyage of the Karluk* he wrote:

The next morning the weather was not altogether propitious, but I felt that to delay any longer was unwise. I went over the supplies with McKinlay, wrote out the instructions to Munro and told the men to keep up their courage and live peacefully and do the best they could. They all wrote letters home which I took to mail in Alaska.

My letter of instructions to Munro was as follows:

Shore Camp, Icy Spit,
Wrangel Island, March 18th, 1914

My Dear Munro,

I am leaving this morning with seven dogs, one sledge and Kataktovik to get the news of our disaster before the authorities at Ottawa.

During my absence you will be in charge. I have already allocated supplies to the different parties. McKinlay has four men, Hadley is with the Eskimo ... which makes four people, Mr Williamson three men, and yourself three men.

McKinlay kindly made out a list for me and I will ask him to give a copy to you, when you get back from your trip to Shipwreck Camp.

You will make a trip to Herald Island to search for traces of the mate's party. On my way I will cover the coast as far as Rodger's Harbour.

The great thing, of course, is the procuring of game. In this Kerdrillo (Kuraluk) will be of great assistance. Let him have his dogs and two others, so he can cover a good deal of ground, and our own parties, scatter them around so that they will be able to hunt and while away the time. Give each party enough dogs, if you can spare them, so that they can better cover the ground.

As we talked about distributing supplies that you bring give each one their proportional share. As it stands now there are 80 days pemmican and oil for each person.

Please do all you can to promote good feeling in camp. You will assemble at Rodger's Harbour about the middle of July where I hope to meet you with a ship.

Sincerely yours,
R.A. Bartlett.

The Captain and Kataktovik left at 8 am. The Captain asked me to accompany him for a bit and talk over things. He gave me the letter for Munro, asked me to help him to the best of my ability. He would have liked to leave me in over-all charge, he said, but since I had no official standing in the ship's company it would be resented by officers and crew. I felt really pleased, though I told him I wouldn't have the job for all

94

the tea in China. 'Canny Scot,' he said with a smile. After about half a mile we said goodbye and they were off, with the hopes and prayers of fifteen people speeding them on their long, lonely journey. On them depended any chance we had of leaving Wrangel Island alive.

When I returned to camp Kuraluk was already busy changing igloos, and I followed suit. The wind had got up again, and it was an appallingly disagreeable job, working in near blizzard conditions. Our bedding was completely saturated before I had finished, but we had to make the best of a bad job, for there was not the slightest hope of drying it until we had a change of weather. I paid a visit to the house which Williamson, Chafe and Maurer were sharing. Williamson and Chafe were slowly recovering from their sickness, but Maurer was now a very sick man. What the trouble was I just did not know. They were blaming the bear meat, but I was sure that was not the cause. Hadley was suffering severely with rheumatic pains. Templeman and Malloch appeared so weak they could do little to help themselves, and Mamen's knee was giving him endless trouble. I was cold, wet and miserable, but slightly cheered at being comparatively fit, for the time being at least. I cooked a meal of minced bear meat, pea soup powder, biscuit crumbs and some Hudson's Bay pemmican, all mixed together in a soup of such richness that when we had finished we had little difficulty in getting to sleep in spite of our extreme discomfort.

Day after day the windy weather continued. Even when we had a clear sky, the driving drift made outside work quite hopeless. We could go out only when it was absolutely necessary, and to spend almost twenty-four hours of every day in cramped quarters, cold and wet and weak, was the ultimate in misery.

Then late one afternoon we thought we heard some animal outside. Thinking it might be a bear, I crawled out, grabbing the rifle, which was near the door. But it was Munro who had returned – without reaching

Shipwreck Camp. They had got as far as the pressure ridges only to find their way barred by an ocean of open water. They had waited three days for a change in conditions before returning. Clam was very sick indeed, and Breddy not much better. All of them had swollen faces. I was puzzling over what this strange malady could be when, in the middle of our meal, Breddy called to me. The roof of the big igloo had fallen in on top of the sick men. We had to move quickly, for they were buried under a deep mound of snow, and in danger of suffocating. We dug them out and moved them to Kuraluk's igloo while we repaired their roof. Only then did we learn that all Chafe's toes on one foot had been frozen four days previously. Although they were not too badly frostbitten, it looked as if Munro and I were the only people, apart from the Eskimos, in comparatively reasonable shape. But oh how I longed for a let-up in the weather. To be out and about and to keep active was, I felt sure, the only defence against a malady that was as much mental as physical.

Munro and I needed that break in the weather so that we could go to Herald Island to look for traces of the Mate's party. Mamen, too, was keen to move; he seemed to be extremely unhappy. We were worried about dog feed. Our fourteen dogs were ravenously hungry; they had been underfed for some time, and were devouring boots, sledge-lashings, harness and anything else left lying around. We had only 104 pounds of dog pemmican left. On a ration of one pound per day that would last no more than a week.

Already the team spirit, which had developed on the trail while the Captain led us, was deteriorating, and quarrels were breaking out over the sharing of food. Biscuits were the first bone of contention. We had five cases of them, each containing 500 biscuits. On my suggestion Munro announced that he was apportioning one case plus 214 biscuits to each party of four, and one case plus 36 biscuits to each party of three; which worked out at $178\frac{1}{2}$ biscuits per man in a party of four, and $178\frac{2}{3}$ in a party of three. This actually, gave each man in a party of three, one-sixth of a biscuit more than a man in a four-man party, but Williamson and Breddy, who were in a party of three, protested vigorously that each party should get one case and the fifth case should be divided proportionately. But this would have given 203 biscuits to each man in the three-party, and only 161 to each one in the 4-man groups. The argument raged

97

for a while, with much strong and obscene language, before Munro's arrangement was accepted with very bad grace.

I know it all sounds ludicrous, and anyone sitting at home with a well-stocked larder will find it difficult to appreciate the angry passions that were roused. But it must be remembered that we were a very small, isolated community with barely enough food to last two months, and many more months, perhaps another year to go, before relief might come. There was a feeling of every-man-for-himself in the air, though it was never allowed to affect the Eskimo children. In the rationing of food they were counted together as one adult, but they usually received far more than half-shares, and even when the food situation was at its grimmest we always saw to it that they had sufficient to eat. Another natural survivor was Nigeraurak, the ship's cat, who always got plenty of scraps, and having no work to do – unlike the dogs – came through the entire affair sleek and unscathed.

Oil was another source of trouble. Some of our cans had spilled or leaked, and though the abundance of driftwood made up for this in good weather, there were the stormy days to be considered, when cooking outside on a wood fire was impossible. There was angry criticism of Hadley and the Eskimos, who were accused of keeping their stoves burning continuously. They were also accused of smoking fresh tea leaves, especially Hadley, and this did nothing to reduce the ill-feeling that had developed earlier between him and some of the others, apparently over some incident that had happened on the trail.

I was beginning to understand Captain Bartlett's plea that I should help Munro in every way I could. He had apparently had a word with Munro, too, on this matter of cooperation between us, for Munro consulted me at every turn, though he did not always accept my advice. Although the Captain had always taken a delight in teasing 'the schoolmaster', it looked as if he was depending on the schoolmaster touch to keep some sort of order among our mixed-up little band. He touched on this when he wrote of me in his book: 'He had a good understanding of human nature – perhaps his experience as a schoolmaster had given him that – and I relied on him to preserve harmony if any question should arise among the different groups on Wrangel Island.'

Of the sick men, Munro, Mamen, Breddy and Hadley were almost back

98

to normal, but Chafe and Williamson were still very ill, and while there did not appear to be anything physically wrong with Malloch, he lacked all vitality and had little interest in what went on around him. The cook, Bob Templeman, was another problem, a potential source of real trouble with his unbridled tongue and capacity for lying. At times it seemed to me that in our very mixed community we had all the seeds of future disaster. In normal circumstances we might have got by as very ordinary chaps, our frailties and idiosyncracies unnoticed by any but our nearest and dearest. A good leader might have brought out the best in everybody – Captain Bartlett had proved that. But on our own the misery and desperation of our situation multiplied every weakness, every quirk of personality, every flaw in character, a thousandfold.

On 22 March it looked as if we might get some more-settled weather, and preparations were made for two journeys. Mamen wanted to move his group to Rodger's Harbour on the south coast, the place where we hoped to be picked up by a rescue ship in July. In my view this was too far away from the main party, between sixty and seventy miles, not counting the inevitable detours in actual travel. Rodger's Harbour would be our ultimate rendezvous, but until the whole camp could move further east I thought some nearer site would be better for Mamen. In the end he had his way. He left next morning with Malloch and Templeman and nine dogs, with half rations for the dogs. Kuraluk went along too. Once they were settled Mamen and Kuraluk would bring back the dogs for a projected trip to Shipwreck Camp.

Munro had now to carry out the Captain's instructions to 'make a trip to Herald Island to search for traces of the mate's party', and it was taken for granted that I would be his travelling companion. We set out with five dogs, taking eight days' rations for ourselves and seven days' half-rations for our dogs; we could not afford more for them. We made a promising start, facing a light easterly breeze, but nine miles out we ran into heavy pressure ridges, running ESE. to WNW. We could not get over these, and we had to head south to get better going. The light breeze freshened quickly to a moderate gale, and visibility was cut to a few yards in the dense, drifting snow. The raftered ice rose to a height of fifteen feet, with hardly a square yard of level ice between. It was a back-breaking business dragging our sledge along; our dogs were really more of a hindrance than a help. After fighting our way for a further six or seven miles we could go no further; we had covered only 200 yards in the last hour. We managed to build a house of sorts, and after our usual tea and pemmican we lay down, so utterly exhausted that we fell asleep at once.

It snowed heavily during the night. Refreshed after a sound sleep, we were away by 5 am, but we were soon in trouble, for the snow was thigh-deep and each step took us only inches forward. Then we were skimming along on smooth ice, in fine weather, with a clear sky and bright sunshine. Almost instantaneously came an incredible transformation – a renewal of the blizzard, with zero visibility and a screeching west wind cutting through us like a knife, at our backs this time. Early in the afternoon we hit ice that was even more difficult than before, and then the same deep, soft snow. Soon we had reached the stage where we could hardly put one foot in front of the other, and the dogs were in an even worse state. We had to stop, and that night was a nightmare of cold and exhaustion.

When we got up at 5.30 am we found that one of the dogs had chewed through his harness and disappeared. The westerly gale was fiercer than ever, but we agreed to battle on, and tramped and tumbled ahead at a mere crawl. About 6 pm we had to admit we could take no more. We could find no compact snow for building, so we sought out a slightly sheltered corner in the lee of a high hummock, scraped together some mounds of soft snow over which we spread a blanket, and under this we crouched, for we could not lie down; and without any possibility of a hot drink, with no prospect of sleep, we waited for the dawn.

Next morning the gale moderated sufficiently for us to brew some tea, and that revived our spirits. We staggered along until about 2 pm when we were stopped by another impenetrable barrier of pressure ridges. It was obvious that the pressure area which had halted us so effectively on our way in to Wrangel Island extended not only along the coast of the island, but continued eastward right to Herald Island. Though the wind was gradually moderating, and the snowdrift letting-up, we decided regretfully to turn back. Even if we and our dogs had been fresh and strong, we two could never have found a way through.

We had travelled on our circuitous route far in excess of the distance between Wrangel and Herald in a straight line, but we were still miles short. The weather had cleared still more and we could see our objective quite distinctly. Climbing one of the highest hummocks, we brought our powerful glasses to bear on the island. If Sandy Anderson and his men had landed and camped on Herald Island, it must have been on the sandspit at the northwestern end of the island. We could see the terrible ridges stretching right in to the island. We could see all along the base of the near vertical cliffs, right up and down the western side. Nowhere could we detect the least sign of anything resembling an encampment, not even on the flattish part of what the chart showed as a sandspit. If they had landed on Herald Island temporarily and then gone on to Wrangel, then they must have been engulfed in the inferno of ice which I was convinced had claimed the doctor's party.

Reluctantly we turned to face the journey back to Wrangel. We had not gone many miles before we were struggling through another blizzard, but we now knew something about the state of the ice, and we worked out a route which took us more quickly to the smoother going. But fierce weather continued and driving into it was utterly exhausting. Darkness closed in, but we were so sure of our way now that we plodded on. Our dogs were so weak they were almost incapable of going forward. One kept falling down, and we had to put him on the sledge. We came across Broncho, one of the dogs Mamen had taken with him (he must have broken loose), and we took him along with us.

It was nearing midnight when we reached camp. After attending to our dogs we made a cup of tea, but we were too tired to eat. We got two items of news: Mamen had quarreled with Kuraluk and had sent him back; and on the way Kuraluk had shot a bear and her two cubs. The second part was good news indeed, but before it could register properly we were sound asleep.

Next day Kuraluk and Munro brought in the three bears. Mamen returned with the dogs that night, reporting that Malloch was very sick. He could give me very little information about the trouble, and I wondered if it was a case of acute depression. Mamen offered no explanation of the quarrel with Kuraluk, except that it had to do with the building of an igloo. We had a rare feed of bear meat and soup, a welcome relief from the nauseating pemmican which had been our staple diet since arriving on the island.

Next day I was very ill, hardly able to move. Apparently I was suffering from the same sickness which had affected so many others. To begin with it felt like a bout of influenza. Every muscle ached terribly, and I was so weak I could hardly raise myself on my elbow. I could not even write in my diary. The weakness might, of course, have been the result of the strenuous ice trip. But my feet got very cold and remained cold in spite of every effort to warm them. When they began to swell, and went on swelling until they were twice their normal size, I knew it was not influenza. It was then I felt glad I had not eaten my ration of condensed milk on the trail. Diluted and warmed that was my only food for several days. The swelling spread to my ankles, but fortunately went no further, and in a week I felt I would like to stretch my legs in the open air. I struggled out, but I was so weak I had to go back inside after a few shaky steps.

On 1 April Mamen left for Skeleton Island, where he had left Malloch and Templeman on the way to Rodger's Harbour. He was loath to go, but Munro insisted that he rejoin the other two. When he had gone Munro, Chafe and Clam set out on another attempt to reach Shipwreck Camp. I gave very little for their chances of getting there, for there was no knowing how far the old floe had drifted. Just before they left a large bear approached camp. He came slowly nearer and nearer, but as soon as he spotted movement in camp he ran off. Kuraluk chased him for about seven miles and got him with his first shot. He killed another bear the following day, and her two cubs as well. Next day he hunted another one without success. The day after, he and Hadley went after six bears in all, and didn't get one of them. And these were the last bears we saw during our stay on the island.

Soon after 9 pm on Thursday, 9 April, Munro and Clam returned without Chafe. They came to the door of Williamson's house where I was living since I had become sick. While they drank tea they told me they had managed to make their way to the north side of the pressure area but could not find any trace of the trail back to Shipwreck Camp. During the month since my last visit the trail on the floating ice pack must have moved many miles to the west. They travelled east and west searching for the trail, then the ice slackened and oceans of water opened up all round them. Clam broke through some young ice up to his waist, and the other two were soaked rescuing him. Then Chafe crossed a narrow lead and before the others could join him it widened, so quickly that they were hopelessly separated. As Chafe drifted away, and the darkness deepened they could neither see nor hear him. On one side were Munro and Clam with six dogs and a sledge containing all sorts of equipment, but no food; on the other side Chafe, with five dogs, a sledge and all the food.

On the morning of 8 April Munro and Clam left the sledge and the dogs and struck south. They spent the night walking up and down to keep warm, and by sheer good luck succeeded in hitting Shore Camp. The soles of Clam's boots were worn almost through and his feet were in extremely bad shape. For hours we took turns at rubbing them and nursing them against our stomachs to try and restore circulation. Munro's right foot was frozen but not so badly and both had severely swollen hands. As for Chafe, well, with dogs and sledge and food he might pull through. After a day's rest Munro had Kuraluk fix up a small sledge out of a pair of skis and went off to find Chafe. It worried me to see him go off alone but I was too weak to go with him, and there was no rush of volunteers.

It upset me to feel so weak and helpless after being so fit all these months. Fortunately all traces of swelling had disappeared; I gave credit for that to the bear meat we had been eating. I had apparently beaten the mysterious malady and I felt I would be restored to strength and well-being if we could have other food than pemmican, which I was certain was at the root of the trouble. Meanwhile we still had some bear meat in stock.

Munro returned at nightfall, quite unfit to go on. Next morning I was able to go out and light a fire, cook some bear meat and brew tea for our morning meal. I moved out of the sick quarters and in with Munro, who had his old igloo dug out sufficiently to accommodate two. We were just settling down to enjoy our tea when a voice at the entrance called out, 'How about some for me?' It was Chafe! And how we rejoiced! But he was in an awful state. His pants were ripped right down and filled with snow. We plied him with hot tea and then he told us his story.

When he was separated from the others he had built a makeshift house, and in the morning he was able to get off his floe and reach the landfast ice. He was lucky enough to stumble on part of the old trail shorewards. His dogs were very weak, so he unhitched them, fed them and camped. Next morning Blondie died and Broncho ran off, so he was left with three dogs. He decided to abandon the sledge with all the food and gear, and carrying his blankets he struck off south. As a precaution he tied the leads of the dogs to his wrist and they led him back through the blizzard to safety – an extremely lucky Charlie!

The profit and loss account of this whole venture was not easy to balance. The immediate loss was obvious – eight dogs, two rifles and ammunition, skins, food, sledges, tools and other equipment. To these had to be added the injuries to our companions. On the profit side there appeared to be nothing, except that the three men were still alive. But Munro had the satisfaction of knowing that he had done his best to carry out his Captain's instructions, to try to get additional supplies from Shipwreck Camp, and make a search for traces of the mate's party. That both attempts had failed could not be held against him, though I just could not understand why he had abandoned the dogs, the rifles and the ammunition. Kuraluk never forgave him for leaving the dogs, one of which belonged to him.

17   *Wrangles on Wrangel Island*

One of Clam's big toes had become gangrenous. It would have to be amputated, at the first joint at least. We had no surgical instruments, only a skinning knife, and a pair of tin shears which we used to make cooking pots out of empty gasoline tins. Engineer Williamson volunteered to act as surgeon. It was a gruesome operation. Two of us held Clam's arms; a third kept his head turned away. Williamson applied pressure to the shears with his knee until they cut through the joint. There still remained some gangrenous matter to be cut away, but this would have to wait until Clam could stand it. I have never known anyone who lived up so well to his nickname; his lips remained tightly closed; there was never a murmur, only a slight twitching of the face muscles. For sheer guts it was incomparable.

Munro and Chafe were still crippled, and it looked as if they, too, might need some surgery, but not immediately. Just to round off a grizzly day, we were all laid low by an outbreak of diarrhoea. The bear meat was blamed. It happened at the end of a four-day spell of wonderful weather, which had done more than anything to help my recovery. It is impossible to exaggerate the uplift it was to our spirits to be able to desert our squalid quarters and be outside in the health-giving fresh air, in glorious sunshine. I remained outside all day and every day. I was still very, very weak, and even when we had only very light breezes I suffered intensely from the cold. But when the air was calm, with bright sunshine, there was a sensation of heat which permeated every fibre of my being. I did all the cooking. I walked up and down for exercise. I took a sledge and hauled it along for about a mile, collected a load of driftwood and built a large blazing fire, round which we sat and drank tea. That became my daily routine. Every step was an effort, every slight exertion exhausting. I wondered when I would ever regain my strength, but my spirit remained high.

Then the fine spell came to an end, and we were once again cooped up in our cramped uncomfortable quarters, once again reduced to eating nauseating pemmican, so nauseating that it took a great deal of will-power to swallow it. But the sun came out on 26 April, the anniversary of the day I had left home, and I found myself full of optimism for the future. Just before I left home our family minister had given me a Bible, with 'Psalm 121' inscribed on the fly-leaf. My Bible was somewhere on the *Mary Sachs* or the *Alaska*, but just the thought of it sustained me, and when I walked along the sandspit and looked at Wrangel's distant mountains, I was seeing my own Scottish hills and remembering those lines from Psalm 121: 'I to the hills will lift mine eyes, from whence doth come mine aid.' My thoughts were not gloomy. I felt that the future held a challenge which was worth meeting, and the thought of facing up to it braced all my faculties, mental and physical. In spite of my weakness, and the diarrhoea, and the pemmican, I finished that day with a feeling of elation, a lightheartedness which greatly surprised me.

Williamson operated on Clam's toe again, cutting away the remaining gangrenous flesh. We were able to attend to the injured outside, near the warmth of the log fire, when the weather was fine. Soon we would have to do all our cooking outside, whatever the weather, because our oil was almost finished. We had only enough bear meat to last two days, so Hadley and Kuraluk set off for the ridge to look for seal or bear. They took our remaining three dogs and their own two rifles. That left us only one rifle in camp since Munro had left the Mannlicher and the ·22 at the ridge the day he got separated from Chafe.

After Hadley and Kuraluk left we had a perfect day. Munro and I went for a walk, or rather, a crawl of three or four miles, which seemed to be my limit. I wanted to join Mamen and Malloch at Rodger's Harbour, but a journey of almost sixty miles was out of the question. Munro wasn't keen for me to leave him. He lived in daily fear of trouble, and I could understand his wanting someone to share the responsibility of keeping the peace in camp. But part of my rations were with Mamen. So was my stock of clothing. The parka I was wearing was torn all down one side beyond repair. Even the lightest breeze blowing through it chilled me to the bone.

When we got back to camp I rekindled the fire. Rummaging in the tin in which we kept the scraps of meat, bone and fat for the dogs, I collected enough to make a pot of broth. We might manage enough for the next two days, and then it was back again to pemmican, unless Kuraluk and Hadley came to the rescue. The weather drove us inside again as April came to an end. The wind was back and it began to snow heavily. I kept up my efforts to ward off the effects of the numbing, stupefying monotony. I chopped wood, cut ice, strolled up and down the spit, cooked when there was anything to cook. Munro joined me occasionally, and we amused ourselves with experiments in cooking, but as the days passed and there was no sign of the hunters, the scraps in the dogs' tin were used up, leaving a residue which our stomachs rejected. We tried experiments with the revolting, unsavoury pemmican, to try and make it palatable, but with little success.

Although I never lost my feeling of inner calm and hopefulness, there were times when the longing to be anywhere but there in that miserable, squalid camp was almost overpowering. I wanted to be alone, and yet, even in the company of all the others, I felt lonely, dreadfully lonely. It might have been better if I could have been with my scientist colleagues, discussing our work, exchanging ideas on subjects of common interest; or even just talking about roses with the Captain. Maybe the 'them scientists' attitude of some of my camp mates was to blame, perhaps some flaw in myself. Certainly whatever was lacking in our relationship was in no way the result of any sense of superiority on my part, for never in my life have I felt as deeply and devoutly humble as I did then. When you're sick, hungry, and freezing in the middle of the Arctic, it's no time to put on airs.

Williamson was untiring in his attentions to his three patients. Munro was almost completely recovered. Chafe's foot was looking much better. Clam's toe was no worse, though it was unlikely to recover fully until he got proper surgical care. One of my hands and my nose appeared to have been nipped, for they were swollen and blistered, with peeling skin, and I wondered if I was becoming careless. Then May opened with a calm and comfortable morning, although the sun was hidden. Everyone was out, sitting chatting round the big log fire. I went off for a four-mile walk, and on my return I built up the fire, boiled water for the cripples' feet and made a pan of tea. Our oil was finished now, and we were completely dependent on our log fire for hot drinks to wash down the dreaded pemmican.

During my excursions in search of wood for the fire I was becoming keenly interested in the variety of the deposits. The bulk of the wood was cottonwood which had probably come from Canada or Alaska, and there was a sprinkling of spruce, which could have come from almost anywhere, North America, Eastern Siberia, or up through Bering Strait. Some of it had probably lain for countless years but there was no sign of decay in it. A fair amount of it showed clear evidence of its civilized origin: some had been chopped, some sawn; some had obviously been dressed in a mill. There was one remarkable piece, about thirty feet long and eight inches square in section. Where on earth did it come from?

One bright spot on our horizon was that the midnight sun was due any day and we had daylight right round the clock. But with the coming of Spring our houses were dripping badly inside and the snow walls were slowly disintegrating. It was really too cold yet for tents, but we had to move into them, for there was no hope of finding snow suitable for repairing our walls. Summer was on the way. Several flocks of birds flew high over-head, and two snow buntings visited us, hopping around cheekily, giving us renewed hope that better times were ahead.

Hadley and Kuraluk had been gone nine days. It was now 6 May, and we were beginning to worry about them. Then Kuraluk returned at mid-night on 8 May, bringing a small seal and reporting that there were three more at the ridge with Hadley. Williamson, who had moved in with the Eskimo family while Kuraluk was away – Auntie was terrified of bears – now rejoined us with a story that Hadley wanted Kuraluk to bring his family and a supply of firewood to the ridge, so that they could settle there for a while. The effect of this news on some of the boys was quite alarming. They declared it was a trick to let Hadley and Kuraluk keep all the hunting spoils. They talked wildly of what they would do. There were threats of violence, even of shooting. I could see it was going to take all Munro's tact and leadership to smooth this lot out.

We had our share of the seal Kuraluk had brought. As a tit-bit we tried frying the liver in a pemmican tin; it was the tastiest delicacy we had enjoyed for a long time. With that and some seal meat we all felt much more content. It looked as if food was all that was needed to mollify the malcontents, though Williamson and Breddy had a noisy quarrel that day. Tempers were really very thin, and I hated to think what would happen if things got really difficult.

May ninth was the brightest morning we had experienced since landing. We sat round the camp fire in the sunshine, discussing, as we frequently did these days, what we would like to eat if we had the choice. The discussion had a little more spice than usual, because there was a good meal in prospect. Our second, and final, portion of seal meat was cut up for boiling, but first we each carved off a small steak, which we fried in a pemmican tin lid. We found, too, that we could cook blubber in a way that made it more palatable. We fried it until it was just beginning to frizzle, when we persuaded ourselves that it could hardly be distinguished from bacon fat. This was beyond doubt a most wasteful use of blubber, but although we were always hungry, we had not reached the stage when we could eat blubber unaccompanied by lean meat. It was a boisterously cheery gathering that dinnertime round the fire, and I hoped it might damp down the pressures that had been boiling up the day before.

I suggested to Munro that he and I take a stroll. I wanted to discuss the situation and find out how he planned to handle it. I said I could not believe that Hadley had any intention of depriving anybody of food, or of taking any kind of mean advantage. I saw nothing unworthy in the plan to remain at the ridge, so long as it remained safe; that seemed to be the only place where there was the remotest chance of securing food. In fact it might have been a good idea for the whole company to move to the vicinity of the ridges, keeping well on the landward side, but with so many invalids it was impossible. The distance was thirty miles out, and thirty miles back. The best plan was to try and maintain some link between the shore and the ridge, so that we might benefit from the hunting.

On my advice Munro had a talk with Kuraluk, and Kuraluk's story put a different complexion on things. He said he was afraid of Hadley, but he was under the impression that Hadley was in charge of the company and his word was law. Hadley's attitude to the Eskimos had always been somewhat contemptuous; he always referred to them in a disparaging way as 'bloody Indians'. Kuraluk said Hadley did no hunting, just went for a walk and then lay in the igloo for the rest of the day. Kuraluk was so scared that he wanted to hurry back to Hadley, as ordered, the very next morning, although he had hurt his back and had been forced to lie up all that day. Munro tried to reassure him, and promised that one or two others would accompany him when he went to rejoin Hadley.

From my diary of 10 May:

The most noteworthy feature of the day was the quick disappearance of much of the snow. During the night there was a strong gale, and in the morning the wind was still high. It was however very mild, and the effect was seen in the black patches now visible along the sandspit and the dark patches on the hills where previously there had been deep snow. ... Kuraluk has decided to go to the ridge tomorrow, and on the following day Munro, Breddy, Maurer and I will go to bring in whatever seals there are. I hope some of the tempers cool somewhat before then, or there will be trouble.

Munro, Breddy, Maurer and I started for the ridge at 7 am carrying, somewhat optimistically, only a mug and a small piece of pemmican. The weather was fine as we followed Kuraluk's trail of the previous day. At 10 am we sighted a dark object ahead and after a mile or two we could see it was a sledge and dog team. When we reached it we found Kuraluk sitting on the sledge, a most forlorn, dejected-looking figure, muttering, 'Me no good. Lost!' He was suffering from snow-blindness, and had lost the trail. We all decided to turn back and arrived in camp in time to share in a piece of bear which Auntie had saved from her ration.

A cold raw morning followed, with falling snow. I went for a walk, though, like Kuraluk, I was suffering from a touch of snow-blindness. It had been pretty well impossible to wear goggles the day before, for they frosted up so quickly that it was extremely difficult to see anything. At 8 am Hadley returned from the ridge, with no meat. Of the three seals left there by Kuraluk he said that only about two-thirds of one remained, but he had not brought it with him. He must have been living high, and the others were understandably annoyed. Pressure was being put on Munro to have things out with Hadley, but Munro was afraid of aggravating the ill-feeling that already existed between Hadley and some of the others, and perhaps making relations worse than they were; so meanwhile he said nothing.

The Eskimos appeared to have some meat left. Perhaps they rationed themselves more strictly than we did, though, in all conscience, it could not be said that we were extravagant. There was, of course, another explanation. When meat was being shared out after the bears were killed, there were parts that were not included in the division – heads, hearts, and the like. These parts were regarded as perquisites of the Eskimos, but they made good eating, and already Auntie had kept us all going for a couple of days on a bear's head which she dug out from her seemingly bottomless store.

Kuraluk's snow-blindness was still acute, but he was hopeful of getting back to the ridge in a couple of days. Munro said he would go with him and bring in the first supply of meat. Munro did have a private talk with Hadley, but this did not satisfy everybody, so there was a round-the-fire discussion at which many problems were given an airing and some doubts quietened. But I had a feeling that the fires of discontent had merely been damped down, not quenched.

Clam's foot continued to improve, but Chafe's had gone gangrenous again. Williamson had done some surgery on him, but he was evidently not being sufficiently severe in his cutting, no doubt to spare Charlie un-due pain. I had some medicines in my kit which I thought might help the invalids, but they were in that part of my kit which was with Mamen at Rodger's Harbour. I had been hoping for a long time to make that journey to join Mamen and now the need for the medicines made me more anxious to be off. But my snow-blindness had worsened. My eyes were extremely painful, and travelling was out of the question, so Breddy offered to go and bring back the medicines.

He returned early one morning, having got only as far as Skeleton Island, where Mamen had camped before continuing south to Rodger's Harbour. Breddy brought a note which Mamen had left for me:

Skeleton Island
24 (27) April 1914

Dear Mac,

I'm leaving this place today for Rodger's Harbour or any other place on the coast suitable. I am going to stay down there, trying to build a cabin, while Bob and Malloch carry the stuff down. If you should happen to arrive in meantime, don't stay here but get down the coast as soon as you can, take with you all you can carry. We have had hard times all the time, no game, illness we all have had and we feel very weak yet. The best regards from Bob and Malloch

Very truly yours,
Bjarne Mamen

I made up my mind I must try to reach them as soon as possible. Why Breddy gave up at Skeleton Island, which was more than halfway, I could only guess. He said the going was extremely tough, but he was one of the fittest of our company, and had taken no part in any of our activities since we landed. I would have to walk all the way, because there were no dogs to spare, and it was a long walk, sixty miles or so. I had no gun, and Breddy had seen two bears near camp at Skeleton Island. I remembered Captain Bartlett's warning against travelling unaccompanied. Yet I had to try, for there was no one else willing to go.

Death at Rodger's Harbour

I left on the morning of Sunday, 17 May about ten o'clock. Munro kept me company for a few miles, unburdening himself of some of his worries, which were very real. Soon after he left me the wind blew up from the northwest. The snow was deep and difficult, and drift reduced visibility to about ten yards. It was about three o'clock the next morning when I reached Skeleton Island. I could scarcely believe I had got so far.

I must confess that the name Skeleton worried me a little. It had an ominous macabre ring, and I had often wondered how the island came to acquire it. (It was several years later before I learned that the skeleton referred to belonged to a whale.) But now I was too exhausted to think of anything but putting up some sort of shelter and getting to sleep. The roof of Mamen's igloo had collapsed. What lay underneath I was too tired to investigate. I found some skins which Mamen had left behind, shook the snow off them, lay down on them and in minutes was sound asleep. My last thought was a hope that none of Breddy's bears would call while I slept

I woke around noon and set off again. I still had twenty-odd miles to go, and I had some doubts about my ability to do it. When I reached Cape Hawaii, the south-eastern point of the island and not quite halfway to my objective, I had to lie down; my right leg was cramping and my left was bleeding through being badly chafed. But I struggled on, and at last I spied a black mark on the beach more than a mile away. Was it a camp? It was! And what a welcome I got!

Mamen's diary, Tuesday, 19 May:

A great joy came to me last night. Mac came down to us at about 9.30; he had come directly from Icy Spit. .... It was a great grief to me to tell him about

Malloch's death. He was still lying inside and a frightful smell came from him. Mac helped me in every way with consoling words to make me forget what I had gone through since we saw each other last, and he succeeded also to chase away the sad thoughts for a while. ... Happily I got out this morning and had a fire lit, and while the water was boiling, we brought Malloch out, rolled him up in the tent cover, laid him out nicely on the ground, put some logs round him to keep the wind out for the time being. That was all we had strength enough to do. Mac said a brief prayer for our departed friend.

My own diary for 18 May says: 'What a woeful state of affairs I found! Malloch had died the previous night, 17 May, at 5.30 pm, after having been unconscious from 9 am. He had had his feet frozen again and, according to Mamen, did not seem to care whether he lived or died. It was not for lack of food, as Mamen said, for the others had been denying themselves to try and keep him up.'

Mamen's diary shows how things had been developing towards the end:

May 14th ... I for my part was out for four hours today, but I don't know whether it did me any good or not. I swelled up frightfully after it, my whole body, yes, how this will end is hard to tell. ...

May 15th ... We have been outside all day. I feel stronger after it, but my body looks horrible, it has swollen up now so that I am frightened about myself. ... Malloch is certainly a peculiar specimen; he told us today that he couldn't see any point in going out and wasting his strength and provisions when nothing could be done. He believes that it does a man good to lie inside all the time without moving. ...

May 16th ... I was up today cooking breakfast, but it was evidently too much for me. I was obliged to go in and lie down immediately afterwards. My body is swelling more and more; my organ looks more like a bull's than that of a man. Indeed I don't know how this will end. ...

May 17th ... Malloch is now beyond hope. I expect he will die any moment. He lost consciousness at 10 o'clock and from that time we couldn't get a word from him. At 5.30 he stretched his legs and drew his last breath, to great grief for Bob and me. I cannot describe how sorry I feel about his death, but I thank my Heavenly Almighty Father that he had such a quiet death without too great pain. He has suffered pain, though, since *Karluk*.

May 18th ... A hurricane-like north-north-west wind blowing snow today, so that we have been obliged to stay inside. ... On account of the weather and our small strength we have not been able to do anything for Malloch. It is not pleasant either for Bob or me, but what shall we do? He is smelling now, too, but we must put up with it until we get better weather. We have not the heart to drag him outside in this weather. I don't know how this will end. Is it death for all of us? No, with God's help we will get out of it. I am still weak but so long as there is life there is hope. There is still something that keeps me alive, all my beloved ones, and with God's help I hope to be home, hale and hearty, and spend Christmas with them. It is two months today since Captain Bartlett left Icy Spit. I hope to see him again in two months time at the latest.

It must have been just an hour or two after he had written that when I arrived. My own diary for 18 May says:

Mamen, too, is in a very bad condition, his body being very much swollen in every part. It is a most curious illness and I cannot understand it. The swelling seems to get worse after eating. The only meat they have had besides one bear ham is a fox which Mamen shot as it was tearing at my bag. It is my opinion that they need a change of meat, and if I have the strength, I intend to take them back to the spit where they have much more chance of getting it.

Next morning Bob Templeman was not feeling well enough to travel, so we had to postpone our departure. I added more protection to Malloch's body to save it from being molested by animals. The ground was still too hard for us to dig a grave, and anyway we had no tools. There was nothing to do but cook pemmican, drink some tea and go to bed. It seemed to me that Rodger's Harbour was a good place for a camp, with every prospect of eggs later when the birds came north. Whether it would afford enough in the way of game for the entire party I could not tell. At any rate Mamen and I agreed to abide by the decision to move back to Icy Spit; it seemed the only chance of his recovery. Mamen's diary continues:

May 20th . . . Mac covered Malloch's grave better today and we made preparations to leave here tomorrow. Bob and I will go with him, for I don't get a moment's peace as long as I am here. Malloch and his staring eyes are continuously before me. My body is frightfully swollen, no pain though. I suppose it will be better as soon as I get away from here, and, with God's help, I hope to have sufficient strength to take me up to Skeleton Island.

May 21st ... The barometer is falling; it now stands at 29·4. In the tent all day, cannot eat now, feel infinitely weak.

May 22nd ... As soon as this weather abates we will make an attempt to reach Skeleton Island, I, for my part, cannot stand it staying here.

Still the weather prevented our departure. When Mamen found he could not eat pemmican I fed him on warmed milk; fortunately there was still a little of my milk ration left; my rations had, of course, been all this time with Mamen. Bob, too, was not in very good shape, but he was at least as fit as I was. On Saturday, 23 May, we were all ready to leave, but Mamen found himself unable to walk. What was to be done? I recalled that among the remnants of my rations which Mamen had left at Skeleton Island there should be some Hudson's Bay pemmican, and I thought the change of pemmican might help Mamen. He agreed, and I set off, taking with me a tin of condensed milk, some tea and matches.

I was only a few miles on my way when I put my hand in the breast pouch of my snow overshirt to get my goggles. The pouch was empty. The case with my goggles must have dropped from the pouch when I pulled the shirt over my head. Not long after, as I expected, my eyes began to cause me trouble. To make things worse the ice scape had changed out of all recognition in the snow and winds of the past few days. I was on the look-out for Cape Hawaii, but must have passed it without identifying it. I went wandering on. I could not be sure in what direction I was travelling, for I was having to make long detours to avoid large stretches of knee-deep water on top of the ice. I was sure I was somewhere along the east coast, for I could see the cliffs. I was being forced farther and farther to the east by the water, which stretched far out from the land. Later I decided that I must have been due east of Skeleton Island, and the immense stretch of water was coming from the first meltings of the river which enters the sea there.

But now I was in a state bordering on panic. It was the only time in all my experience, on the ship, in the ice-pack, on the island, that I felt fear; not fear of danger, but from the weight of my responsibility to Mamen, the helpless frustration of being lost while he waited for me to bring help. Even now, sixty years later, I can recall the sensation exactly; it still makes me feel ill and desperately unhappy. I had simply no idea of my exact whereabouts. My eyes were becoming more and more painful and useless.

Hours later I found myself in deep snow; to the southeast, a few miles away, I could dimly see the outline of a bold headland. I must have passed beyond the limits of the east coast and turned westwards, and was now somewhere near the lagoon on the north coast, wandering on the foothills. I had lost all sense of time and direction. I set a course which I thought must take me on to the sandspit, and hours later, wandering and stumbling, I recognized the black pebbly patches from which the snow had cleared. I lay down on the bare pebbles, utterly exhausted. I had crawled over forty miles as the crow flies; how much more I had travelled in detours and attempts to find my way, I could not even guess. To retrace my steps was out of the question. I decided that I must be about fifteen miles from Shore Camp and my wisest course was to go on there and get help.

I arrived about 4.30 am on 25 May. My boots and stockings and legs were soaked through, well above my knees. The soles of my boots were worn into huge holes. Where the holes were the skin was gone, and my feet were raw and bleeding. No other trip I made compared with this one for sheer torture. It was the penalty of ignoring the Skipper's advice never to travel alone in these parts.

I roused Munro and gave him a very brief report before falling sound asleep, just as I was, wet and miserable. Later in the day I made a full report on the state of things at Rodger's Harbour. It was obvious I would be off the active list for some time, and it was arranged that Munro and Maurer should go down at once, see what conditions were likely to be later in the season, and if they considered them favourable, return and remove the entire party south. They had to postpone their departure for a day because of heavy snow, and they left on 26 May.

When they had gone I had a long, hard think about this terrible illness that had taken poor Malloch and laid Mamen so low. Williamson was now swollen up like Mamen, though not so badly. Auntie, too, was complaining of swollen legs and ankles. I realized now that my sickness after the Herald Island trip had been the beginnings of the same trouble, and that I had been saved by my milk diet, followed by the bear meat. I was now convinced that our pemmican was to blame for this strange disease.

So was Stefansson. Commenting on Hadley's account of our experiences on Wrangel Island he wrote in *The Friendly Arctic* (pp. 717, 718):

The pemmican was not only insufficient as a ration, but led to illness of both men and dogs. That does not mean that there was anything poisonous about it. It is merely an illustration of the generally accepted fact that a diet consisting almost entirely of protein leads to 'protein poisoning', which is poisoning in the sense that illness results, because the kidneys are overtaxed with trying to excrete the excess of nitrates. This leads to nephritis or derangement of the kidneys, of which a common symptom is swelling of the body, beginning at the ankles. Our pemmican makers had failed us through supplying us with a product deficient in fat.

There is not the slightest hint anywhere in Stefansson's book that he accepted any responsibility, as leader, for the deficiency of the pemmican, which was our staple diet, and which led to so much suffering and loss of life. It should have saved our lives, not taken them. In his *Secrets of Polar Travel* Admiral Peary wrote:

Of all foods I am acquainted with, pemmican is the only one that, under appropriate conditions, a man can eat twice a day for 365 days in a year and have the last mouthful taste as good as the first. And it is the most satisfying food I know. I recall innumerable marches in bitter temperatures when men and dogs had been worked to the limit and I reached the place for camping feeling as if I could eat my weight of anything. When the pemmican ration was dealt out and I saw my little half-pound lump about as large as the bottom third of an ordinary drinking glass, I have felt a sudden rage that life should contain such situations. By the time I had finished the last morsel, I would not have walked round the completed igloo for anything that the St Regis, the Blackstone or the Palace Hotel could have put before me.

And Peary added: 'Next to insistent, minute, personal attention to the building of his ship, the Polar explorer should give his personal, constant and insistent attention to the making of his pemmican and *should know that every batch of it packed for him is made of the proper material in the proper proportion and in accordance with his specification.*' (Author's italics.)

The day after Munro and Maurer left for Rodger's Harbour, Kuraluk returned from the ridge, bringing part of a seal with him. It gave us a pot of rich soup, but little more. Two days later he shot a seal which gave us meat and soup for three days. But it was about this time we realized we were no longer enjoying the one luxury left in our lives – a good cup of tea. The bottom of the tins in which it was brewed had become so worn that the tea turned black and had a most peculiar pungent taste.

The swelling complaint was spreading. Clam was the latest victim with ankles and legs beginning to swell. Williamson was getting worse, but my rest was having a beneficial effect, and it looked as if I might escape another bout of the illness. I had all along felt that my mental attitude was more important than any physical weakness. I knew I must expect a spell of bodily weakness until we could get fresh meat, but I also knew that the limit to which my body could be driven had not yet been reached. Breddy and Chafe had joined the sick list, but it was not clear just what was wrong with them. I had an unhappy suspicion that sometimes it was a case of what became known a few years later as 'malingering'. Indeed I felt sure that a little more activity in the keen but not unkindly air was all that was needed to cure them.

Munro and Maurer had not returned by 2 June, which worried me a little. Kuraluk had decided that he and his family would move to Skeleton Island, since our present location offered little or no prospect of food, now that bears no longer came around. Hadley wanted to go too, and it was decided that I would accompany them next morning and bring back the sledge and dogs. We were away by 8 am, Kuraluk breaking trail, and Hadley handling the sledge. Auntie, the kids and I walked along the spit. We made good progress, covering about six miles by 10.30, but I could not keep up, even with the children, and fell far behind. I was longing to stop, but I felt that if I could not keep going I might as well give up altogether, so I kept going and managed to catch up when the others stopped to brew tea and eat a bit of pemmican. I spied a seal on the ice at Bruch Spit, but neither Kuraluk nor Hadley had seen it before it disappeared. Still, it was a welcome sign.

About 4 pm we reached the end of the spit, having travelled thirteen or fourteen miles since morning, and we pitched the tent. We cooked some deer hair in a blubber soup and fed it to the dogs. For us there was the usual pemmican, fried in blubber. Whatever awful things it was doing to us, we had to eat it. It was all we had. But this was the last of some Hudson's Bay pemmican that Auntie had, and it tasted a little better than the Underwood variety. Helen and Mugpi stewed an owl they had found dead – from starvation, it seemed from its meagre condition. We were now within easy distance of Cape Waring. Next day we could cut across the foothills and reach it some time during the day.

We were wakened at 1 am by Munro and Maurer with bad news. Mamen had died, on 26 May at 5.30 am, before they had arrived, and three days after I had left Rodger's Harbour. Mamen's diary entry for 2 May, which finished, 'I for my part cannot stand it staying here' was his last. All he managed to write the following day was the date, 'Saturday, 23rd May.' Although the news was not unexpected it still gave me a terrible shock. The last of my scientist colleagues had gone.

Munro and Maurer had promised Bob Templeman that they would return to Rodger's Harbour. Munro's idea was that I should stay with the main party, but we should move camp to a little bay near Cape Waring. There was plenty of driftwood on the beach, and tens of thousands of crowbills were nesting on the cliffs south of Cape Waring. They had shot twelve with the Mauser pistol.

Munro wanted me to make for this new camp with Hadley and the Eskimos, then take the sled back to Shore Camp and transfer the sick and wounded to the new camping ground. Then I was to go to Skeleton Island and bring back whatever gear there was of any use. I thought this was all a pretty tall order, especially without consulting me, and I must admit I was pretty annoyed at Munro. But he was in charge and I had promised Captain Bartlett I would support him, so I said nothing.

Munro and Maurer were continuing to Shore Camp to collect the rest of their gear before settling in at Rodger's Harbour. When they left, at 3 am, the rest of us got up, breakfasted at four, and were on our way by six. We reached the new camping ground at 9 am and we were just brewing tea when a flock of geese flew overhead. Kuraluk brought one down with his rifle, and by the time the water was boiling the goose was plucked and ready for the pot. After a gorgeous meal of stewed goose Kuraluk and Hadley were off to the cliffs for a raid on the crowbills. Kuraluk returned with a very small young seal which he had shot on the ice. He also had six gulls; he had seen no *aatba* (crowbills). On went the pot again, and part of the seal was cooked for supper. While we were eating Hadley returned with ten more gulls. So was founded our new home, and as Genesis has it, 'There was corn in Egypt.'

On 6 June the Eskimos were up at 5 am but I lay in as I intended to start back to Shore Camp in the evening, and I was certainly not feeling equal to it. About 1 am we had tea and some soup, scraps of gull, seal and blubber left over from breakfast. Then I had my first smoke in many months, – a cigarette made from the bark and leaves of a small ground plant found on the flat land in the neighbourhood. None of us could identify it; Hadley thought it might be a very stunted form of Arctic willow. The paper for our cigarettes came from the leaves of one of Hadley's freemasonry books, of which he had several. All the Eskimos were suffering, more or less, from snow-blindness; they seemed to be more prone to it than the rest of us. Kuraluk and little Mugpi were worst.

We had supper about 6 pm and I started off immediately afterwards. Before I left, Auntie cooked me a gull to eat on the trail, and she gave me seven gulls, one for each man at Shore Camp. I kept the breast and a leg of my bird to give the fellows a foretaste. When I arrived at 1 am everyone was eager to know if I had brought any meat. When I showed them the gulls they did not appear very enthusiastic. They seemed to have a prejudice against eating gull, but after I let them have a taste of my cooked gull they changed their attitude pretty quickly and could hardly wait to have their birds cooked.

Before I left the new camp Hadley and Kuraluk had invited me to move in with them when I got back. I reckoned that they had seen how difficult life had been for me for so long, and that it was likely to be even more so if Munro was going to move to Rodger's Harbour and leave me behind. I said I would wait until I had consulted Munro, and he offered no objection when I saw him at Shore Camp. He was anxious to get moving, so I suggested that I should take the sledge with all the gear half-way to the new camp, and then return for Clam and Williamson, who would have to be carried on the sledge. The others would walk along the sandspit at their own pace, erect the tent and have everything ready for me when I arrived with my invalids. Munro agreed, and I left after breakfast. I covered about eight miles before unloading. I turned right round and was back in Shore Camp by mid-afternoon. After a cup of black tea, I settled my two sick passengers on the sled, and was off again within half-an-hour. It proved a very heavy load for three dogs, to say nothing of myself, for there had been no let-up since leaving Waring Camp the previous evening. It was the all-round-the-clock daylight that made it possible. We arrived at our halting-place only to find, to our disgust, that the others, who had arrived on foot, were sound asleep. I had to move the two sick men unaided, unhitch and feed the dogs and brew a cup of tea. I turned in at midnight in no very amiable frame of mind.

I was very loath to get up when Munro called me at 8 am. I made a meal, for the dogs, of bear fat, seal skin and blubber, and some deerskin cut from a worn-out pair of my socks. After tea and pemmican Munro and I set off on the second half of the journey, taking Clam as passenger with the tent and some essential gear, and leaving Williamson with the rest of the gear to be taken later. Munro and I had an argument on the way about the route. Tempers were beginning to wear thin, my own unfortunately included. I had a nagging notion that Munro and I were losing accord with one another. I felt that his decision to go to Rodger's Harbour alone was an abrogation of his responsibility, and I was feeling 'let down'. Then I saw something which restored my equanimity. Here and there small patches of the ground had been cleared of snow, and while we were deep in argument my eye lit on a small pool of colour on one of these clearings. It was a patch of a lovely little wild flower, which I could not identify, a purple patch striking in its contrast to the surrounding white wilderness. Even more remarkable, so remarkable that I got down on my knees to look more closely, was the fact that the edge of the snow had been undercut by the wind and the little plants were alive with colour for quite a distance under the snow.

The argument ceased; my spirit was uplifted, my mood transformed, my outlook changed, not only then but for a long time to come. Thoughts of death had been uppermost in our minds these recent days, but here was proof that life could still triumph in this bleak landscape. I arrived in camp with feelings of renewed faith and hope.

There I found more mundane things to bolster my morale. Kuraluk had shot a large seal, and Hadley ten crowbills. It was 8 pm and soon we were enjoying a meal of underdone seal meat. This was the way the Eskimos preferred their meat, and I had to admit that it was much superior to our over-cooking. It had an entirely different flavour. I lay down for half-an-hour, and about 9 pm the walkers arrived – Breddy, Chafe and Maurer.

Then I was off to fetch Williamson. The dogs were so tired that they could hardly pull the empty sledge, so instead of enjoying a ride I had to crawl along, as tired as my small team. When I arrived about 2 am Williamson was sound asleep. I woke him up, and while he was eating the seal meat I had brought him, I made tea, loaded the sledge, fed the dogs and was ready to start by 4 am. At first the sledge skimmed along at a fair pace, but I had trouble from the many pools of water that had formed with the melting of last year's ice. Some were bottomless holes, covered with a very thin crust of ice which the dogs and sledge broke through as we rushed across. The dogs disliked the water intensely, and on one occasion, as they hesitated, the whole outfit crashed through the ice and the sledge slid down into the water at a dangerous angle.

Then Nigger and Mollie broke their traces, and while I was trying to catch them, Unguluk got away. Off the three of them sped in the direction of camp. Williamson thought he might try to walk, supported by the handles of the sledge, while I hauled it, but after fifty yards he could go no further, and I was certainly in no fit state to drag him on the sledge. I suggested that I should pitch the tent over him and go back to camp for the dogs, but Williamson preferred simply to lie on the sledge. I laid him on top of a sealskin, a heavy deerskin and two fawnskins, and I wrapped around him two blankets, a travelling rug and the tent cover. Then I set off to walk the ten miles to camp.

The snow was beginning to soften as the temperature rose, and I trudged on, sinking now to the knees, now to the thighs. The light was bad and my eyes began to give me trouble. At last I reached camp, exhausted and half-blind, to find that the dogs had returned and Kuraluk had gone back with them overland an hour before. He returned in the early afternoon with Williamson, who was none the worse for his experience. Meanwhile I had moved into my new quarters with Hadley and the Eskimos to enjoy my first rest for three days.

But Munro had other ideas. He wanted me to accompany him and Maurer to Rodger's Harbour, bring back the dogs and sledge and then call at Skeleton Island for the Mauser pistol and whatever other gear there might be. For the first time I really lost my temper with Munro, but the outburst didn't last long. I was now suffering the effects of the worst attack of snow-blindness I ever had, and I was too miserable to care what happened. I was totally blind and suffering acute pain; the temptation to rub my eyes and ease the feeling in them of being full of sand and grit was overpowering, but it had to be resisted at all costs.

Munro was not inclined to wait for my recovery, but I was not much interested. He set off with the intention of taking Breddy with him to do my job, but Breddy was away hunting birds at the cliffs, so Munro and Maurer left on their own. For a time my eyes kept me helpless. Hadley did his best to alleviate the pain by injecting cocaine and bathing them with zinc sulphite, but the relief was little more than momentary. I had to lie with my eyes bound up and had to be led, and even fed. I swore that never again would I go out without my goggles, for one of the drawbacks is that every attack predisposes one to other and more severe attacks.

Kuraluk and Chafe had a good day at the cliffs, returning with forty-one crowbills. These were divided between the two tents in the ratio of five to four; although there were six people in our tent, the two children were reckoned as one, but in fact they each ate as much as any adult. During the night we were wakened by groans from the other tent, followed by shouts from Williamson that he could not breathe. The others got him outside and called Hadley, who found Williamson sitting on a log with the fear of death on his face. Williamson complained of his heart, but

Hadley recognized the symptoms of acute indigestion. It transpired that each of them in the other tent had eaten two crowbills and shared two gulls. Hadley gave him some medicine and we went back to our tents. Another crisis was over, but it was apparent that the rationing of food was going to be just as much trouble when we had plenty of food as when we had practically none.

I was impressed by the way in which the Eskimo woman made the meat ration spin out in our tent, compared with the extravagance of the four men in the other tent. They had finished their birds while we still had eight or nine left, enough at least for one more day. The difference lay in the fact that we cooked only one bird each per meal and drank tea with it, saving the juice, which we boiled up later, with seal blubber and some seal blood. Thus we had another meal at mid-day with rich soup. The others all ate two birds each per meal and drank all the soup, so they had two meals where we could stretch to three, or three and a bit. It could not be called fat living, for with no other solids, one crowbill was not a large helping; but I found our rationing fairly satisfying, and with the uncertainty of the future, I felt we were playing things a little more safely.

At last 1 was able to remove the bandage from my eyes. It was a joy to be able to eat my evening meal without help, picking my bird to the last scrap of meat. Hadley was suffering from swelling in his legs, but as it was accompanied by acute pain I reckoned it was something other than our mystery disease. The next night he was able to go to the cliffs, followed by Chafe and Breddy. Time was of no significance; there was no darkness and night had no meaning. Breddy returned about an hour later, and I heard him report that there was not a crowbill to be seen, but that he had shot one gull. It seemed that the crowbills left the cliffs at intervals, remaining away for a day or two; the absence of open water in the neighbourhood of the cliffs drove them to more distant feeding grounds.

About 3 am Hadley got back with ten gulls, and I went to join him in a cup of tea. Tea was back in favour again; we were using a five-gallon gasoline tin, and we kept it filled with a brew which we simply put on the fire to heat whenever we felt like it. Chafe did not return until about 7 am and we heard him report having four gulls. But when his tent-mates came along later to ask about breakfast, they told us Chafe had only got two gulls and said nothing about Breddy. Hadley was very worried indeed. He foresaw serious trouble if this sort of cheating continued.

My eyes were almost back to normal, and I started for Skeleton Island, taking with me a cooked crowbill for the morning. I wanted to take the Mauser pistol with me, but Williamson refused to let me have it because, he said, Munro had given orders that it was to remain with their group. Hadley's opinion was that this was intended to prevent Kuraluk having the use of it; Munro and Kuraluk were still not on good terms since Munro had lost one of his dogs. Poor Munro seemed to be in bad odour all round, which might account for his keenness to be at Rodger's Harbour. I certainly did not blame him for that. I would have liked to have been there myself.

So I travelled to Skeleton Island, once again unarmed, and I just had to hope that I would not meet an aggressive bear on the way. When I reached the island I found that Munro had moved most of the gear, but I brought back what was left – 270 rounds of Mauser ammunition, my own bag, 1 empty biscuit tin, 1 empty coal oil tin, and 7 tins of pemmican. My bag had been thoroughly ransacked and many of my belongings were missing, among them two Jaeger caps, a sack of boot packing, a notebook, several pairs of Jaeger socks and my compass.

Hadley and Kuraluk made full use of every break in the weather to go after the birds. When the crowbills were gone they got gulls. Chafe added a few with the Mauser, but with a great waste of ammunition, and Hadley was convinced that he and his mates were still cheating about what they shot. I was by no means idle, as it fell to my lot to attend to the chores for both tents. I would have welcomed the opportunity to join in the hunt for food. The few occasions on which I had a chance to use a rifle convinced me that I had an eye for shooting (and two years later, during World War I, out of a company of 200 officers and NCOs, I received one of the only two distinctions in musketry).

But there was nothing I could do about it. After Munro had lost the rifles at the ridge we only had two rifles left, and it was only reasonable that these should be left in the hands of the two experienced Arctic men, Hadley and Kuraluk. There was one other rifle, Hadley's own, a ·401 Winchester, but this was useless now because all its ammunition had been blasted away. At Rodger's Harbour Munro had a rifle which had belonged to Mamen.

One day when I was alone in our tent I heard steps outside and looking through a small hole in the wall I saw Chafe and Breddy helping themselves to our soup. Breddy then handled the birds in our store, and when I checked on them they were one short. I said nothing, and when Hadley and Kuraluk returned with forty-three crowbills we divided them as usual in the proper ratio, nineteen to them and twenty-four to us. After supper the others turned in, but I had to stay awake to attend to Clam and Williamson, since Chafe was at the cliffs and Breddy was resting for a projected trip to Skeleton Island. Clam was much better, but Williamson declared that he was much worse. He was talking of giving Clam another dose of morphine, but Hadley who had a stock of medicines would only give the dose after a written request from Clam. Two or three days later Clam was back for more and got half a grain. Clam said this had no effect, and Hadley gave him another dose. But first he made him write a note accepting responsibility for any ill-effects. And that, said Hadley, was to be the last.

June seventeenth was the anniversary of our leaving Victoria. It was a perfect day; the sun shone with a brilliance that I have never seen surpassed anywhere, and the temperature inside our tent was 82° F. To save ammunition Kuraluk was making a bow and arrows to hunt the crowbills. We were hoping soon to go gathering eggs, but that would be a difficult and dangerous job, because of the height and ruggedness of the cliffs. We had found two places where we thought a man might be lowered from the top, and that job was likely to fall on me, the smallest and lightest in the party.

Hadley and I went some way up the foothills to assess the prospects for sealing and far away in the distance we thought we saw land, bearing about ENE., away beyond Herald Island. Two days later it showed up again quite clearly. If it was land it was something new and uncharted. Of course it was not uncommon for explorers to see what they thought was land and find later that it just did not exist. But in this case the outline remained so constant, day after day, that we felt sure it must be land and decided to christen it Borden Land, after Canada's Prime Minister. It has long been established that such land does not, in fact, exist, but Hadley and I derived a great deal of distraction and satisfaction from our observations.

About 1 am we heard a noise coming from the area where we built our fire, and we came tumbling out of the tent to find Munro and Maurer cooking ten crowbills which they had shot on the way from Rodger's Harbour. They ate the lot there and then! Munro said there were a great many ducks around Rodger's Harbour, but he was short of ammunition and wanted Hadley to hand over 50 rounds. This was going to give him, counting what he still had left, 170 rounds for three men, while Hadley and Kuraluk would be left with only 146 rounds for ten of us. What a row there was! But Munro was in charge, and in the end Hadley had to hand over the 50 rounds. That meant we could no longer afford to shoot birds. Our ammunition would have to be conserved for larger game.

Munro denied having given any order that I was not to have the use of the Mauser. He also said that the articles which I had missed from my bag at Skeleton Island were still there when he left. Who was the thief and the liar? Was it Munro, or was it Breddy?

Our visitors slept all day without having visited the sick men, and when they woke up and were having breakfast, Breddy appeared and demanded in very strong language that they visit the other tent. Hadley and I were asked to join them, and what a meeting there was! All the pent-up ill-feeling of months erupted in a flow of charges and counter-charges. The language was loud and obscene. It was almost impossible to make sense out of the barrage of words. Breddy and Williamson were demanding that everyone should come back to stay at Waring Camp, and help take care of the sick and forage for food. If that were not possible, then Maurer at least should return.

When Breddy demanded Maurer's return he said that I should be the one living at Rodger's Harbour, but Munro retorted that I had no wish to be there. Munro knew this was untrue. I could not have wished anything better than to be at Rodger's Harbour, away from all the moaning and whining and suspicion, but Maurer had persuaded Munro to let him go there, and Munro was in charge. I was a mere passenger in this ship's company, without any authority; as Breddy seemed to take a delight in reminding me, I was 'just a bloody scientist' But I could not let Munro's falsehood go unchallenged, and I am afraid I lost my temper again. I also lost all desire I ever had to accompany him.

Finally it was decided that Munro and Maurer would go back to Templeman at Rodger's Harbour, but as soon as the water had cleared off the surface of the ice, I would take the sledge and dogs and bring the three men back to the main camp. I had a feeling that Munro had no intention of returning, and sure enough he called me aside and suggested that I should not seriously attempt to reach Rodger's Harbour, but just take the team part of the way and return with a report that the journey was impossible.

I was furious. If he had no intentions of returning, I told him, he should face up to his responsibility and tell everyone. I said I would report his suggestion to Hadley, but would say nothing to the others to avoid aggravating an already ugly situation. Hadley duly recorded the matter in his diary.

But when Munro and Maurer had left I began to realize that perhaps the arrangement was all for the best. Very shortly the journey south would become impossible, and during all the arguments about who should be where for his own comfort and convenience, everyone seemed to have forgotten one crucial point. The Skipper's last sentence of instruction to Munro read: 'You will assemble at Rodger's Harbour about the middle of July where I hope to meet you with a ship.' Transporting the entire party south was quite out of the question. If Munro, Maurer and Templeman joined us at Waring Camp, Rodger's Harbour would be empty, except for two graves. If a relief ship called, unless Munro was able to leave a message, our rescuers would have no idea where to find us.

It would be nice to think that this was what was in Munro's mind all along, but I felt certain that in face of the more immediate problems of staying alive, he had forgotten that part of his instructions, otherwise he could have quelled the row at the outset by reminding everyone of the need to have someone at Rodger's Harbour. Perhaps I ought to have reminded him of it, but I was so disgusted with the whole business that it did not occur to me until later. No harm was done. For the right reason or the wrong, Munro would be there to meet any ship that might come.

We now had to face the very serious problem of finding subsistence for at least two months, and probably longer, with a very limited amount of ammunition. Captain Bartlett's estimation of 'the middle of July' was, I was convinced, a very optimistic one; the middle of August at the earliest was much more likely, and it could well be later. Our 140 rounds of ammunition would not carry us that far, unless we were fortunate enough to get nothing but large game. And we had to face the possibility that a ship might not be able to get through before the ice closed in again; or that the Skipper might never have reached civilization. Then we would have another winter ahead of us. But that prospect was too awful to contemplate.

Hadley and I made a bosun's chair in which I was to be lowered from the cliff-top in an attempt to get eggs. But first we made a ladder and went off to see if we could reach any nests from the bottom of the cliffs. I was a bit worried about my legs which were swelling behind the knees and numb. There was the niggling thought that it might be a return of 'the disease'. I was suffering from stomach trouble too, and I blamed the pemmican. We had a little of that left and had been using it to eke out our meagre diet of birds.

We seemed to be too early, for many of the nests of the small gulls were empty. The ledges on which most of the birds were nesting were seven or eight feet higher than the top of our ladder. In my efforts to reach them I almost came to grief. Standing on the highest rung of the ladder I grabbed hold of a projection on the cliff face to hoist myself higher. As soon as I took my feet off the ladder several pieces of cliff came away, including the piece in my hand. I fell with the rocks hurtling after me, but with my usual good luck they missed me, and I landed in snow before rolling on to the hard ice, bruised and shaken but all in one piece. We only got ten eggs from about a hundred nests, and Hadley unwisely squandered a few precious cartridges on gulls, shooting four; but one of them landed on a ledge which we could not reach.

Unfortunately the kind of diet we were getting made me in no condition for such mountaineering exploits. The strain of carrying the heavy ladder, the struggle with the cliffs and the shock of my fall left me completely unable to get up the next day, but I could not afford the luxury of idling for long. I faced the journey back to Shore Camp to bring back the gear that had been left there. The ice was becoming very rotten and would soon be breaking up for the summer. I had to get the journey over before conditions became impossible, so I started out after a day's rest. The ice was even worse than I had expected. There was no continuous surface. Last summer's ice cakes were separated by lanes of water which had been the young ice of the winter, now melted. It was impossible to tell which of these lanes might be a treacherous hole going right down to sea-bottom. The remaining ice cakes were mushroom-shaped. The sledge had to be dragged to the top of each huge mound, steadied, and then allowed to run down the other side, usually crashing into the dogs who were hesitating on the brink of the next lane of water. On one occasion sledge and dogs landed in the water, dragging me with them; a piece of ice projecting from under the water saved the whole outfit from going completely under. It took a lot of effort to pull myself, then the dogs and the sledge on to the ice, and I continued the journey with much more caution. Later I came within twenty yards of a large seal asleep on the ice, but I had no weapon. Thank goodness it wasn't a large wide-awake bear!

When I had collected the gear and returned to Waring Camp that evening I felt satisfied that I had made my last ice-trip for the season. I dare not think what Bob Bartlett would have said about my wanderings on the ice, alone and unarmed.

Kuraluk arrived just behind me with fourteen birds that he had shot with his bow and arrows. Hadley had thirty birds but they had cost twenty-five rounds of ammunition. We were desperately in need of larger game before our ammunition ran out. Every day a keen lookout was kept for seals. I spotted a large one about 250 yards from the beach, but it kept disappearing into its hole, and re-appearing only when the hunter moved away.

There are three methods of hunting seal, depending on the conditions in which they are found. If they appear in an open lead the aim is to put a bullet through the brain and try to get the seal before it sinks. Sinking is much more common in summer, partly because the seal is less fat and therefore of greater specific gravity, and partly because the water is less dense, with the melting of the surface ice diluting the saltiness of the sea-water.

Having killed a seal you have to secure him. If you can't get close with a kayak, you use a *manak*, such as the Eskimos used when we were on the *Karluk*, to throw beyond the floating carcass and drag it to the edge of the ice. If the seal is lying on the surface of a large expanse of ice there are two methods of killing it. You can find his hole, settle down beside it with harpoon and line, and prepare to practise infinite patience. In winter the hole may be a mere breathing-hole, and the seal may have several such breathing-holes to choose from; so you may have to wait three or four days before his snout just shows, and then you must strike quickly.

In and around summer, when he is in the habit of basking on the ice, waiting for him to appear is not such a long business. On the other hand you may decide to stalk your seal while he is lying on the ice, and this demands a greater degree of skill than any other method. In his book, *My Life with the Eskimo* Stefansson describes the results of observations which he made with Dr Rudolph Anderson on the habits of the seal in these circumstances. The seal's basking is apparently not an unbroken, continuous period of sleep, but a series of alternating periods of sleep and wakefulness, allowing him to guard against the approach of his main enemy, the bear.

Stefansson and Anderson found that the periods of sleep varied between 2 and 100 seconds, and of wakefulness between 2 and 10 seconds. The average sleeping period was 30·1 seconds, and the waking period 4·5 seconds. The secret of successful stalking lies in long study of these habits. You may be able to approach within about 300 yards of the seal without being spotted; beyond that you must begin to act like another seal. When your quarry raises his head and looks round he may see you and become suspicious. If you remain still too long he will decide that you are no seal and disappear. So you must imitate his sleeping and waking routine, raising your head at the end of the maximum period of sleep, and looking around for the maximum period of wakefulness, until his suspicions are allayed. Then you may be able to approach near enough to get in a killing shot.

But there is another obstacle to be overcome. His constant coming and going, out and into his hole, has worn a slight incline in the ice around the edge, and even if your shot has killed him, he is liable to slide down the slope into his hole and be lost. So before shooting you must be close enough to run forward and grab him before he disappears.

You have to be very hungry to go through this long, complicated, and slightly ridiculous process. And we were very hungry. Every day Hadley went out after that big seal I had first spotted in the middle of the smooth bay ice. Every day he appeared and every day Hadley stalked him: but he always spotted Hadley at about fifty yards distance, and down his hole he went. At last Hadley got near enough to fire and hit him badly, but the seal managed to slip away. On the way back to the beach Hadley noticed a seal coming up in a crack which ran along close to the beach. One shot was enough, and when he was fished out he proved to be our old friend; he had two very pronounced wounds.

That was 23 June and we had been subsisting on birds since 8 June. These had provided us with very meagre feeding indeed, and that night we enjoyed our first satisfying meal for a fortnight – a good helping of underdone seal meat with fresh blubber, and luscious seal soup, flavoured with fish, for the stock had been enriched by boiling the seal's stomach, and it was full of tomcod, a small fish about the size of a sardine.

In our tent we had enough left from our share of the seal to last us four days, and enough birds for another day. But the fellows in the other tent had no birds left, and that night they fried liver and cooked far more seal than we did. Hadley had spoken to them repeatedly about their extravagance, but they refused to take his advice, even now when the last morsel of pemmican had been eaten. In all fairness it has to be said that by any ordinary standards they were not being gluttonous, but our circumstances were far from ordinary. By Stefansson's reckoning 'a party of three men and six dogs need about two seals per week'. We had one seal in fifteen days for eight men, one woman, two children and three dogs.

The behaviour of the four in the other tent was certainly worrying, but far worse trouble was brewing there than any of the rest of us suspected. Very soon our little company was to be shattered by another tragedy.

June twenty-fourth brought a violent south-easterly gale, and at 5 am I had to crawl out and re-erect our tent, which had been blown down on top of us. I cooked our remaining birds for breakfast, plus a pirate gull which little Helen had killed. She had fastened a piece of blubber to a feather quill, to which she attached a piece of string, anchored by a stone. When the gull swallowed the blubber the quill stuck in its gullet. Helen and Mugpi shared the victim, on top of their breakfast ration of gull.

The other tent had finished their seal meat at breakfast, and they were grumbling about the previous day's share-out, though Hadley always made sure that they were present when Auntie cut up the meat, and at the time they had seemed satisfied with their ration. Now they were threatening all kinds of trouble, including keeping to themselves all they shot with the Mauser. Breddy and Chafe went off to hunt birds and eggs and returned with five birds and two eggs. True to their promise they made no suggestion of sharing and cooked the lot for their supper. Or was it breakfast? At times we were in doubt as to what meal we were eating. We were out and about in the eternal daylight sometimes for more than twenty-four hours. Then we might be asleep throughout what would normally be regarded as daytime. The only way we could check was by referring to our diaries.

On the morning of 25 June I woke about 6.30 am when Hadley was going out of the tent. I must have fallen asleep again, because I was suddenly wakened by the sound of a shot. I stuck my head out of the tent, thinking Hadley had fired at a duck or something. But then I looked round and saw that Hadley was lying in his usual place in the tent. Then I heard Williamson shout, 'Clam! Call Hadley! Breddy has shot himself!'

I was up and out in a flash, before Clam was out of his tent, and I was followed by Hadley and Kuraluk. Breddy was dead. He was lying in his tent, the Mauser revolver beside him. Clam and Williamson were asleep, they said, and were awakened by the shot, Chafe was away hunting. The bullet had entered the right eye, penetrated the brain, and emerged on the left side of the head, a little above the ear, and higher than the point of entry.

Was it an accident? Did he commit suicide? If he did, then what had gone on in the other tent to drive him to such a desperate action? Or was it just that he could not face the prospect of many more weeks, perhaps another winter on the island? We would never know the answers.

We carried Breddy outside, and in the presence of everyone, Williamson went through his effects. All the articles that had been taken from my bag were there, including my compass, which was hidden in a sock. During the day Kuraluk and I did our best to dig a grave at the top of a small hill behind the camp, using an axe to break up the frozen earth and a piece of board for a shovel. After supper Hadley, Kuraluk and I improvised a stretcher out of three poles and a piece of canvas and carried Breddy up the hill. His body had swollen so much that the grave was not deep enough. It was extremely difficult to get down any deeper without proper tools, because we were now down to the permafrost, which was much harder than the frozen surface earth. I spent the next day at the deepening, and at last we were able to lay Breddy to rest, covering him with a heap of driftwood, over which we laid skins and piled soil and moss, to keep out animals.

Life went on. While I was digging Breddy's grave at the top of the hill Hadley and Kuraluk were hunting as usual. Hadley missed a seal, and then sat at the hole all day, waiting in vain for him to show again. But Kuraluk brought in a seal he had shot two days before, and we had a really satisfying meal of blood soup, made in the Eskimo way and quite different from the concoctions we had previously been calling blood soup. Auntie's way was to cook the seal meat and remove it from the pot, but leave the pot on the fire so that the liquid kept on boiling. Blood was then carefully and slowly trickled in so that the pot never went off the boil, and all the time stirring had to be kept up continuously. When enough blood had been added the boiling and stirring were kept up for a little longer. Then the pot was taken from the fire and the soup allowed to cool slightly. The result was fairly thick, rich and highly palatable. I slept soundly after that, and even managed a smile when Williamson woke me in the middle of the night to ask me to make a cup of tea for him and Clam.

Hadley had taken custody of the Mauser and the Winchester rifle, which were his own personal property, and also of the ammunition belonging to them. Only twenty-four revolver cartridges remained, and three of the original hundred rounds of ammunition for the rifle. As he put them away, Hadley remarked that he wasn't going to have any more accidents. Chafe had been out at the cliffs and returned with two birds, both of which Williamson at once handed over to us. He admitted that they had been cheating on birds. For example, the previous Wednesday Chafe had reported two eggs and four birds when, in fact, he had six eggs and five birds. Williamson also admitted that Breddy had stolen birds from our store. I was tempted to tell them how the American explorer, Greely, handled the situation at Cape Sabine when twenty-four of them had to face a winter of 250 days with only forty days' rations; he had not hesitated to sign the warrant for the execution of one man caught stealing seal thongs, which were all they had to eat. But Chafe and Williamson seemed subdued, even contrite, so I let the matter drop.

As the end of June approached we began to feel that better times were ahead. According to my diary: 'June 27th was the most beautiful morning we have had, without a cloud in the sky. Our tent was so warm at midnight that we could not sleep until we had opened up the front of the tent.' I was busy collecting material to protect Breddy's grave when I was startled by a fusilade of shots. I was sure Kuraluk had bagged a bear, but, no, he had been firing at a seal, twelve shots in all – and it got away. But he shot another one later.

Hadley and I had another go with our ladder, lengthened now to ten feet, and consequently heavier and more unmanageable than ever. The only fastenings we had for the joints were lashings of sealskin thongs and these quickly worked loose. It was impossible to make them rigid enough, so the ladder kept sagging at the joints and threatening to collapse completely the higher I climbed. Still, we did collect twenty-one eggs. I had a shot at the crowbills with Hadley's revolver and got three. When we arrived back in camp we found that Kuraluk had caught a Pacific Eider duck which could not fly. So we all had two fried eggs each, and the duck for supper – quite a rewarding day.

But next day our hunters drew a blank, and when we got back to camp Auntie told us there was not a scrap of meat left. Everybody rushed out again, and Hadley eventually came back with a Pacific Eider duck. We were so hungry we cooked and ate it before turning in. Kuraluk did not return until the middle of the night and he woke us up with the news that he had killed two seals. In the morning Helen and I went out with him to bring in the carcasses. We had to walk fourteen miles and I began to be aware again of my extreme weakness. I had not walked more than very short distances for a long time, and this journey made me acutely conscious of the effect malnutrition was having on me. I had just got back with the seal, when I spotted Kuraluk, with my glasses, dragging in another. Out I went again with the sledge and dogs. Then dense fog stopped hunting for the day.

Three seals might seem an abundance of meat, but not when divided among seven men, one woman, two children and three dogs, with absolutely nothing else to eat. June was coming to an end and it was difficult to assess our prospects. The period of crisis was approaching. I could not truthfully say that we had at any time been reduced to starvation, but we had been very hungry, very hungry indeed. My main worry was the very poor return we were getting for a very great expenditure of ammunition. Meat was around, but it was proving extremely costly to acquire. It was no exaggeration to say that our lives depended to a great extent, though not entirely, on our ammunition. To quote Stefansson, 'When we are stationary, it is possible to average better than 125 pounds of meat to each cartridge.' I doubt if we attained even one per cent of that average.

To make matters worse Kuraluk, who was our mainstay as a hunter, chose this time to demonstrate a not uncommon characteristic of his people: there was meat in camp, so there was no need to worry. He lay back – and the month of July was to prove the worst in our experience. Fog settled down in what should have been high summer, and in the intervals between the fog we had heavy rain, day after day without ceasing. The imminent break-up of the ice, leaving large stretches of open water between us and the ice, was going to make hunting even more difficult unless we had a boat. Yielding to continuous pressure, Kuraluk at last agreed to build a kayak.

The only tools we had were a hatchet, a snow-knife and our skinning knives. From the hatchet-head Kuraluk improvised a reasonably serviceable adze, and with this he roughed out the sides and ribs of the frame from two large logs. Then, with our skinning knives, we whittled these down to their finished form. It was a real joy to me to find satisfaction in this work. I don't pretend that it demanded any skill on my part; all it called for was patience, and of this I had an inexhaustible fund.

Then suddenly Kuraluk seemed to lose interest. For a whole week he did no work on the kayak. Indeed, when we moved our tents a few hundred yards along the beach to get a cleaner environment, the kayak frame was the only thing left on the old site. It was not until the bay ice broke up and drifted out of the bay altogether that Kuraluk took up his boat-building again. He even spent one of the wettest days working outside in the rain, putting the finishing touches to the framework, lashing all the separate pieces together with sealskin thongs. Then followed three more days of inactivity. When I pointed out to him as tactfully as I could that we needed food, he told me that he had no fear of starving as long as there was blubber. We had quite a good store of that, but I am afraid the prospect of existing on blubber alone, even for a short time, had no attraction for me.

A long rainy spell got Kuraluk going again, fashioning the double-bladed paddle and scraping the sealskins which would cover the framework. Sixteen days after beginning the job, we brought the frame inside the tent and Auntie sewed the skins together over the frame. The following day, 19 July, it was successfully launched.

All this time Hadley was untiring in his efforts to get food, much more so than Kuraluk with his reluctance to hunt until necessity drove him. In view of the controversy and criticism which developed in later years over Stefansson's theories about 'living off' the Arctic, I summarize here the records of our two hunters in the two months of June and July. In June Kuraluk fired at eleven seals, killing five common seals and one bearded seal, and missing five common seals; in July he shot at six seals, bagged two common seals and three bearded seals, and missed one bearded seal. In June Hadley shot at nine seals and retrieved one common seal, missed seven common seals and one bearded seal; in July he fired at ten seals, getting four common seals, and missing five common seals and one bearded seal. The bearded seal is between five and six times heavier than the common seal.

This record shows that the total number of seals fired at in June was twenty, and in July, sixteen. In *The Friendly Arctic* Stefansson states: 'A good hunter should get sixty or seventy per cent of the seals he goes after.' Translating our figures into percentages we get for Kuraluk in June, fifty-eight per cent, in July, eighty-three; for Hadley, in June, eleven per cent, in July, forty. But these figures are somewhat inflated because they refer to the number of seals at which the hunters actually fired, and take no account of the many more seals which were stalked, but escaped before the hunters could get a shot in.

My analysis is not intended in any way as a criticism of the skill of either Kuraluk or Hadley. It is a simple illustration of the game conditions on Wrangel Island, and the actual achievement of men desperately trying to keep alive by hunting, as against a theory of what ought to happen, or what happened to someone else under totally different circumstances.

About the middle of July another potential source of food began to appear – the walrus. I think the walrus is the ugliest creature I have ever seen. A fully-grown one may measure ten or eleven feet long, and weigh between one and two tons, with rounded head, small, beady black eyes, huge tusks about two feet long and coarse, stiff whiskers. Its huge flippers, broad, flat and webbed in front, and fan-shaped behind, look clumsy and cumbersome, but the walrus is remarkably agile at pulling itself from the water on to the ice. It is almost as valuable to the Eskimo as the seal. The meat is nutritious, the tough hide provides cordage and covering for canoes, and the ivory makes perfect spear-heads.

Kuraluk was extremely scared of hunting walrus, especially in a single kayak. He knew what Nansen was talking about when he wrote, 'Any moment we might expect to have a walrus tusk or two through the boat, or to be heaved up and capsized.' But in spite of his fears Kuraluk went after walrus. Day after day he remained out in his kayak from morning till evening, and on 20 July he got his first walrus – and his only one as it happened. It was only a baby weighing less than 1,000 pounds, but even so we had great difficulty hauling the ungainly carcass on to the narrow strip of grounded ice along the beach. My first meal of walrus meat was excellent. 'Tasted like roast beef,' I wrote, but I think I wrote the same about bear meat. Hungry as we were any meat tasted delicious.

Even when we were reduced to living on the walrus hide I still found it highly palatable. Well boiled, the inner lining resembled a jelly mould, about one-and-a-half inches thick, but it required prolonged and vigorous chewing before it could be swallowed. On several other occasions a few of these monsters came near the beach. Day after day we could hear their lion-like roars. Much later we saw a herd of many hundreds floating on top of the floes as they drifted north. They would have provided an excellent haul for walrus schooners, but we never managed to catch another one.

On three separate occasions during July there was trouble over the sharing-out of meat, and in each case Hadley or Auntie calmed things down only by handing over part of our reserves. The egg market had closed. Only once during the month did we enjoy the luxury of a boiled egg. In a walk over the foothills Hadley had stumbled across an eider duck nest with a full complement of six eggs. He brought home five of them, leaving one in the hope that the mother would not forsake her nest. Our boiled egg, however, turned out to be more duckling than egg.

We had one very small but agreeable addition to our diet. On one of my walks I found a small plant which had a familiar look. It resembled sorrel, or what in my boyhood days in Scotland we called 'sourocks'. I tried chewing a leaf or two and found it had a familiar acidy favour, so I gathered some and took it back to camp. Everybody liked it. Hadley knew it at Point Barrow as 'scurvy grass'. It was not very plentiful and grew only in the small runnels made by the melting snow earlier in the summer, but I kept on collecting it, and we were never without a supply.

But July was a hungry month, and we were often close to starvation level. We ate tails and flippers which had lain around in our meat tin for so long that they were rotten and disintegrating. At times we were reduced to chewing sealskin and walrus skin. We had a fair supply of blubber, but only when there was absolutely nothing else to eat could I force myself to swallow it. Taken along with lean meat I could enjoy it, but alone it was disgusting. I was glad when we were able to use seal oil instead of blubber. The Eskimos conserved it by storing the blubber in a sack, or 'poke', which was made by skinning a seal in a certain way.

The first cut is made round the mouth, then, working the knife round underneath the skin, the Eskimo peels the skin back inch by inch until the whole skin is turned outside-in like a sock.

The tail joint is severed in such a way that the whole skin can be removed in one piece, a perfect bag, with a circular hole at the top. It is dried and cured and turned right-side-out, and stuffed with blubber cut into small pieces. The hole at the mouth is then securely tied and the poke is left lying outside until all the blubber is converted into oil and goes sour. Into this we dipped whatever we had to eat, whether it was lean meat, sealskin, deerskin or walrus hide, before putting it into our mouths. It was slightly more acceptable than the raw blubber.

I kept busy on wet or foggy days trying to mend my clothing, which was so rotten that the skin would not hold stitches. I was much worse off than the fellows in the other tent, who had never been as active as me, so their clothing had never had to stand such hard usage. Hadley and the Eskimos were best dressed of all, because they had been much better equipped originally with their own outfits of clothing of the highest quality and workmanship. The outlook was bleak for me if we were forced to winter on the island, for we had no skins suitable for making clothing.

But we were not too worried about the future. We were taking things fairly philosophically. Our interest in the weather and its effect on the ice was concerned mainly with the prospects for food. We had not yet reached the stage of questioning the success of Captain Bartlett's mission, although the middle of July had passed. This unconcern might have continued if the weather had allowed us to get out and about. But on 'a day of thick fog' with 'nothing else to record', my diary shows the first sign of worry about the future: 'On such an inactive day, our thoughts turn to the future. Now that time is wearing on anxiety begins to creep in. When will relief come? Will we be relieved this season? Or must we winter? God forbid! For our chances will be slim. Only patience!'

Hungry July ended with a feast. Kuraluk shot an *ugruk* (the large bearded seal) on the twenty-ninth, another on the thirtieth and a third on August first. Nothing as wonderful as this had happened to us since killing the bears back in April. Great care was taken in the skinning of the *ugruks*, for it is their skins that are used in the making of the *umiak*, as well as for boot soles. We might need a skin boat one day and we would certainly need new soles on our boots if we were here much longer. We were by now quietly preparing to face another winter, so that if a relief ship did not turn up we would not be completely unorganized. We erected a meat rack, on which a portion of the lean meat of the *ugruks* could be hung to dry. We had even tentatively fixed on a site for a winter hut, where Kuraluk had found an abundance of driftwood and thought game prospects might be good.

There was now trouble between Hadley and Kuraluk. Hadley had killed an *ugruk* in the water in front of our tent, but it sank before Kuraluk could reach it, as his kayak was lying further down the beach. According to Hadley's diary:

> Shot and killed an oogruk and the native went out to the place about 100 yards from the Beach and cast his Drag a few times and then quit, and come in and said that he could not find it. If he had shot it himself he would have found it, if it had taken him 6 hours to do so. He is getting almost unbearable the fault of some of them praising him continuously they have given him the swelled Head and spoiled him.

On 8 August he wrote:

> Saw plenty of walrus on the Ice but our Kayak Expert was too scared to go to

them and we Lost a good chance 2 Large walrus was feeding all day yesterday about 500 or 600 yards off round a Large ground cake of Ice a fine chance for a man with a kayak – – – but with our man nothing doing another fine chance for meat Lost I think if we have to winter here that we shall be up against it [And the following day:] August 9 – – – I Shot a walrus today that was feeding about 300 yards from the Beach I put 2 shots in him and hurt him so bad that he Tried to get on the rocks but he could not but he sunk about 20 yards from the Bluff I was standing right over him and see him sink but the native came and Looked with his kayak and Stayed there a few minutes and says he could not see him the water was to Dark and then went Back apparently he Dont want any meat that he do not kill himself.

Hadley decided that he would shoot nothing now unless he was able to recover it himself.

Now our attention was fixed more and more on the state of the winds and ice. My diary entry for 10 August:

South wind still blew strongly when we turned out and continued all day. The edge of the pack was many miles off from our bay so that it was barely visible with the naked eye. Our hopes were high that this wind would bring the ship, but the native, who went to the high land above the Cape, reported that the ice was close to the land all along the east coast, working and crushing badly. That now is our only thought in our waking moments – when will she come? Will she come? Was the Captain lost? Only time will give the answers. But God forbid that we should have to winter here; it is a hopeless proposition. Nothing doing today but picking grass.

On 12 August Hadley wrote:

Plenty of water Ice going north all the Time we Expect the Ship here at any time now without something happened to the Captain and he never reached Siberia – and in that case we will have a pretty Hard time to get out of it. But we will have a Try for it anyway. We will have a try for Siberia next April if we can pull Through until Then with 80 cartridges to find grub for 12 people.

Although I kept as active as I could I was becoming more and more conscious of my physical weakness. Every step was taken by sheer effort of will. I could not have walked to Rodger's Harbour, let alone to Siberia. What worried me even more than the steady decline in my physical well-being was an increasing sense of loneliness. My difference with Munro had shaken me badly. I had nothing in common with my companions in the other tent except our common distress; my only contact with them was when they were engaged in argument with Hadley over food, and I felt I no longer had any influence with them. At times I felt weighed down with weariness, wretchedness, and an anguish which I knew I must keep in check.

Then gradually it dawned on me that I had been concentrating on the purely material and had lost sight of what had previously been my mainstay – that inscription in my Bible, Psalm 121. At once my spirits lifted. It was not simply that I stopped worrying about the future; it was an acceptance of the fact that the future was not in my hands. It was the acceptance of 'Thy will be done'. I was still acutely conscious of my depressing physical weakness. I was still determined to do all in my power to counter it, but the wretchedness of spirit was gone. I felt much more contented. I was ready to face whatever was to come.

Keeping in mind the need to conserve ammunition Kuraluk tried every method his native skill could contrive to get food. He killed a bird or two with a spear. He practised with a 'throwing' stick, but without any luck. When the ice filled the bay there was nothing, not a living thing to be seen. A large flock of geese flew over one day, but all we had of them was the sound of their flight. On 26 August Kuraluk saw the tracks of a bear. On the twenty-eighth Hadley and I saw a pod of five walrus far out on the ice, but when he and Kuraluk went up the hill to pinpoint them they were gone. Everything seemed to be against us.

Hadley, Kuraluk and I were determined to do everything possible to preserve our supply of dried meat intact, for it seemed our only insurance against starvation. But we had still to put up with the improvidence of our colleagues. One day when we three were out of camp they tried to persuade Auntie to give them some of our walrus hide. They had finished theirs a week before. Their share of the three *ugruks* – half the catch, although they were only three to our six – would last them only three more days, and they had made no effort to preserve any of it. Our share was still drying on the rack. It looked as if we would have to keep them going on our ration.

Then Williamson suddenly announced his intention of visiting Rodger's Harbour. We were absolutely astonished. He had never walked a mile from camp since the day we landed on the island. Yet he set out on the morning of 18 August and returned on the morning of the twenty-first. It just did not make sense that a man who had been inactive for so long should be capable of covering between sixty and seventy miles in that short period. I could not have done it at that time. He reported that the three men at Rodger's Harbour were all well and in good spirits. They had had five seals and a large number of duck eggs, but were now living on sealskin. The ice was still around the south coast, but as Williamson was leaving it had started moving under the influence of a south-west gale, and Munro was not expecting a ship before the end of the month. Williamson brought back a ·45 Colt revolver and 36 cartridges belonging to the cook. Hadley wrote in his diary: 'I told him he had better not have any more accidents with guns in that Tent because I would not stand for any more.'

In the eternal search for food the Eskimos had introduced a new item to our diet, the roots of a plant unknown to us, long and fibrous, and looking and tasting like what I, as a boy, had known as 'liquorice stick'. It had to be boiled for a long time and required a great deal of chewing. With this and scurvy grass and the rotting scraps from our meat tin, we continued to keep our dried meat intact. What we ate had little or no sustenance in it, but it prevented the violent muscular contractions of an empty stomach and deadened the sickening hunger pains. But the liquorice root also gave us acute constipation. In spite of plenty of seal oil, our bowels simply ceased to function. In fact my entire internal mechanism seemed to be in complete disarray.

On 22 August Williamson asked for some of our precious dried meat. Hadley noted: 'Meat all gone we started on our Dried meat and that will soon be gone we've to feed both parties now with it and then we will start on the skins.' We decided to give each man in the other tent a daily ration which would not be increased under any circumstances. In return we asked for a share of their tea tablets; ours had been finished for some time, but they still had plenty, because they had the remainder of the rations of Munro, Maurer and Breddy. I had never recovered my ration from Mamen, so Munro had a good supply at Rodger's Harbour. Williamson had brought back 300 tablets from there. He gave us 88 tablets, and while we drank our first mug of tea Hadley grimly announced

146

that from then on he would 'prove as good a horse-trader as the next fellow!'.

Since I had gone to live with Hadley and the Eskimos the routine at mealtimes had never varied. We all sat round with the dish in the middle and helped ourselves, dipping each morsel in a separate dish of seal oil. This practice did not, of course, ensure an equal distribution. If one happened to be a slow eater it was just too bad. Now, as we started on the dried meat, Auntie started to divide it up at each meal and give us separate portions. When the meal was over we noticed that each of the Eskimos kept back a little from his or her plate and put it in a closed tin. Hadley and I were intrigued, and his reaction was typical of his attitude to the Eskimos – 'I'm damned if I'm going to let a dirty Indian beat me, even at saving meat!' So we both started a savings bank of our own. However, just when I had saved enough for one meal my tin fell off the meat rack and the dogs got my savings.

We tried to eke out the dried meat by having meatless days. On those days a typical menu was: Breakfast, a mug of soup from the rotting scraps in our 'starvation' tin; lunch, a mug of tea with a piece of walrus hide and some decomposed blubber from the 'poke'; supper, cooked roots with tea. But I finally decided to give up roots. My digestive organs could stand no more.

For four weeks after the killing of the three *ugruks* not one living thing fell to our hunters. On 28 August the ice was back in the bay and we were scouting round hopefully. Here and there were a few pools of water in which crowbills were swimming around with their young. We could not afford ammunition to shoot them, but Kuraluk had a brilliant idea. Why not net them? We dug out a net which had lain neglected under a snowdrift. With infinite care we disposed ourselves round a hole filled with birds and with a mighty heave cast the net over them. Not a bird escaped us. Our first day's catch was 30 old birds and 60 of their offspring. The following day we got 120 all told. We were jubilant. The haul was not to be compared to an *ugruk*, or a walrus, or a bear, but it was such an unexpected windfall, and all achieved without the expenditure of a single cartridge. Our spirits rose. We forgot for the time being that August had ended and hope of rescue had dwindled almost to vanishing point.

September opened fine and fair, with clear skies, bright sun and a very light southerly air. Kuraluk killed thirty crowbills with his throwing stick. Hadley sat at a seal hole for hours and was just about to give up when the seal's snout appeared. He killed it, but it sank like a stone, and Kuraluk refused to try to find it. Hadley tried to grapple for it himself and he managed to bring the seal to the surface, but before he could get his hands on it, it slipped off the hook and disappeared.

It was bitterly cold next day, but Hadley sat at a seal hole all day, and the day after, becoming more and more despondent. Sitting beside a hole for six hours on end with nothing happening was a depressing occupation. There was not a sign of any living thing, except the odd young fox. There were several of these around from time to time, quite unafraid and very inquisitive. They would sit watching us at a distance of not more than ten feet. If we made any move towards them they would trot off, stop when we stopped, then turn and resume their watching. Williamson fired thirteen shots at one little fox with his Colt ·45, and at the end of the barrage the fox was still sitting staring at him.

We were hungry, almost desperately hungry. Our birds were finished, our dried meat was gone, and sealskin could do no more than stave off starvation. We caught one young fox in a trap, but it merely proved tantalizing. Hadley said that foxes were not usually eaten, because they were too rank in flavour, but I could find no fault with that little fellow. I kept busy making and setting traps, not just for meat, but also for skins. I was optimistic enough to think I might get enough to make a fur shirt for the winter.

We were now having heavy snow again, and we were all doing what we could to improve our clothing, though some of us had little hope of keeping warm. Kuraluk went along the beach and cut off a large slab of whalebone from part of a skeleton he found. With this he intended to shoe a sledge which he would build during the winter for use on our long journey to Siberia in the spring. What optimists we were!

By 6 September we had decided that there was no prospect of bigger game in the area and we would move next day to our new camp site and start building a hut for the winter. That afternoon Hadley and Kuraluk returned dragging a seal. It was a mere infant, not more than enough to provide one main meal. Unashamedly we gorged on seal meat and blood soup, stifling our conscience with the excuse that we would be fitter for the strenuous work of moving house next day. And we finished off the banquet with a helping of fish, the first we had caught during our stay on the island. Auntie and Helen had seen these small tomcod, about fifteen inches long, in a crack in the beach ice, and caught them by 'jigging' for them. The jig was merely a bent pin fastened to a length of sinew. This was lowered into the crack and held stationary until a fish swam over it. Then, with an upward jerk, the fish was impaled on the pin. They caught about two dozen, and they were so delicious that we decided to get up early next morning and go 'jigging' for our breakfast before the big move.

So, at daybreak on 7 September everybody in our tent was out with a bent pin on the end of a line, and the tomcod catch was slowly piling up. After a few hours we three men returned to the tent to get on with preparations for the removal. Then Kuraluk went out to find a piece of wood to make a spear for Hadley. He was hardly outside when he startled us with a mighty shout:

'*Umiakpik kunno!*' ('Maybe a ship!')

Hadley and I tumbled out, and I got my glasses on the object which was causing Kuraluk's excitement. It was three miles off to the east, at the edge of the ice which filled the bay and beyond. And without any doubt it was a ship, a small schooner. She seemed to be steaming northwest, and we could not tell whether she was a relief ship, or just a walrus-hunter chasing the large herd we had seen on the ice a few days before.

When we saw her hoist her sail our hearts missed a beat. She wasn't looking for us! She was on her way north! As one man we started shouting, and the noise must have scared every seal in the Arctic, though I doubt if anyone heard it three miles away on the ship. Hadley blazed away precious ammunition with his revolver, and we sent Kuraluk racing over the ice in the hope of heading her off.

Then we saw her lower her sail, and as we watched, hardly able to believe our eyes, a party of men disembarked on the ice and began walking towards the beach. We were saved! Captain Bartlett had got through!

We were in a daze. Stupified by shock and disbelief, we could only think of one thing – food. We called to Auntie and the kids and found that they had collected about two pounds of tomcod. Keeping our camp routine to the last, we traded some of the fish with Williamson for tea tablets. As our rescuers were crossing the ice to reach us we were putting on the pots for a meal of fish and tea, determined to eat our tomcod before we left. We didn't rush out with glad cries to meet the men who trudged up to our tents. We were shy and too dazed to speak. It was all so unreal, like a dream. We shook hands, and they told us they were from the schooner *King and Winge*. They were on their way to trade and to hunt walrus, but their owner, Olaf Svenson, had promised to look for us if he could get near enough Wrangel Island. They had called first at Rodger's Harbour and had Munro, Maurer and Templeman on board.

Obediently we stood and posed for a cinematograph cameraman, who had joined the *King and Winge* in the hope of a rescue story. He followed us everywhere as we stumbled about, gathering our bits and pieces together. We left our tents standing, with conspicuous notes fixed on poles in case any other search vessel should arrive. (In fact the *Corwin* managed to reach the island not long after we left.)

We staggered out across the ice for the last time. We were sure we could walk unaided the three miles to the ship, but the cameraman insisted that each of us should be supported by two of the ship's company. I think it made a better picture. The men told us that Captain Bartlett had organized a rescue operation after reaching Siberia, and he was now on the United States Revenue Cutter *Bear*, which was also making for Wrangel Island.

Someone told us that all the world except the United States was at war, but the news made almost no impact on our reeling brains. We were more interested in the prospect of the meal waiting for us when we got on board the *King and Winge* at 1.30 pm. This was something we had been dreaming about for months. A thousand times we had imagined how we would relish those first mouthfuls of real food. It would be a memorable meal. But it was nothing like that. We ate mechanically, still in a dream. The first thing I ate was bread and butter, but when we had finished our meal I could hardly remember what I had eaten.

Then came a hot bath, and that really was luxury. There was no use pretending that one bath could move all the dirt and grease caked on different parts of our bodies; it would take many soakings to do that. But we did feel cleaner when we donned new clothing from the ship's 'slop chest'. We mooned around, or lay down on beds of skins spread on the deck. We got up again and drank coffee in the galley, where the coffee pot was kept continuously bubbling on the stove for our special benefit. We smoked and smoked. We lay down again, got up again, drank more coffee. Sleep was impossible.

During the short night we tied up to an ice floe, and at 4 am we got under way again. The ice had thickened up, but strangely enough the risk of being frozen in again never crossed my mind. After a great deal of bucking and twisting and turning, we reached loose ice and steamed towards Herald Island. We wanted to make one last attempt to look for traces of the Mate's party. But we came up against ice which was solid and impenetrable, and we could not get near the island.

At 11.30 am on 8 September, as we turned southwards, we spotted the smoke of a steamship, which was coming towards us. It was the *Bear*. She hove to, and as she came alongside, we saw a familiar figure on the deck. It was Captain Bartlett.

After Captain Bartlett and Kataktovik left us on 18 March at Icy Spit they found travel very good at first, all along the lagoon and down the east coast. The snow was hard and windswept, but gradually the swirling snowdrift cut visibility down until they could not see a dozen yards ahead, and they had to camp near Skeleton Island. When they had built their igloo and were about to make their tea, they discovered a hole in their tea boiler. Captain Bartlett mended it by plastering it over with some chewed-up ship's biscuit.

Next day conditions were still bad. The only living things they saw were a raven and a lemming. There were no bear tracks, old or new. When they had rounded Cape Hawaii and reached the sandspit at Rodger's Harbour, the Captain was satisfied that neither of the two missing parties had landed anywhere on that part of the island. He had intended to cut across the ice due south from Rodger's Harbour but found the way barred by high raftered ridges. They had to travel the whole length of the south coast, right to the extreme south-west point of the island, Blossom Point, before beginning the journey across the ice-covered Arctic Ocean to Siberia.

Twice their sledge was broken in the rough ice. It was a ceaseless struggle to get around, or across leads of open water, the most exasperating and treacherous of all Arctic travel. This was the time when Munro and I were making our attempt to reach Herald Island. Howling gales from the west, and then from the east, were bad enough for us, travelling on grounded ice; they were on moving ice, and Bartlett had to use all the arts and skills he had acquired in his father's Newfoundland fishing and sealing business, and on the many Arctic trips he had made with Peary.

Stefansson had only a small fraction of Bartlett's experience of the drifting pack, and I cannot find anywhere in his records evidence that he ever encountered conditions like those that Bartlett and Kataktovik faced in Long Strait. The Skipper told me that he had never met with such ice in all his long experience.

Every device known to explorers – bridging, ferrying, relaying – had to be used, and many others known only to Newfoundland sealers. The gales wrecked their igloos and buried them and their supplies under deep snowdrifts. Kataktovik was afraid of the drift ice and had to be encouraged, even bullied along. The whole dog team broke loose while they were seeking a way across a lead, and in a body the dogs went rushing back over the trail. Bartlett was almost in despair, afraid they would not stop till they got back to Wrangel Island, leaving him stranded halfway to Siberia. But the dogs did stop, to rest, and he managed to grab the dragging traces.

Even when they sighted the Siberian coast forty miles away they still had to force their way through a barrier of pressure ridges only slightly less formidable than the one that had faced us on the approach to Wrangel Island. After that came the deep snow, and then, at five o'clock on 4 April, seventeen days after leaving Shore Camp, they set foot on Siberia, near Cape Jakan. They had travelled more than two hundred miles.

They followed a sledge trail and came up with a party of Chukchee. Kataktovik was terrified that the Siberian Eskimos would kill him, but the Chukchees were delighted to see them and eager to offer hospitality, though neither Bartlett nor Kataktovik could understand a word they said. They unharnessed the dogs and fed them, and put the sledge into the outer compartment of their house. An old woman pushed Bartlett on to a seat, brushed the snow off his clothes, pulled off his boots and stockings and gave him a dry pair of stockings, pulled off his parka and hung it up to dry. The same was done for Kataktovik.

Captain Bartlett wrote:

Here we were, clad only in our bearskin trousers and seated comfortably about a large wooden dish filled with frozen reindeer meat, eating socially with twelve or fourteen strangers to whom, it might be said, we had not been formally introduced. Never have I been entertained in a finer spirit of true hospitality and never have I been more thankful for the cordiality of my welcome. It was, as I was afterwards to learn, merely typical of the true humanity of these simple kindly people.

During the two days they spent with the Chukchees, sheltering from a blinding snowstorm, Bartlett and Kataktovik mended the tears which the jagged raftered ice had made in their clothes, made new dog harnesses and repaired their battered and broken sledge. One of their hosts offered to accompany them as far as Cape North and Bartlett was delighted.

I knew now [he wrote] that with luck I should be able to reach civilisation and arrange to have aid sent to the men on Wrangel Island. I thought about them all the time, however, and worried about them; I wondered how the storms which had so delayed our progress across Long Strait had affected Munro's chances of retrieving the supplies cached along the ice from Shipwreck Camp and getting back safely to the main party, and how the men would find life in the island as the weeks went by.

As he continued his sledge journey across the northern tip of Siberia, heading for a point on the east coast opposite the coast of Alaska, he met with the same overwhelming hospitality at every *aranga* (Chukchee house) along the route. They also met some Russian traders, and one of them gave Captain Bartlett a letter of introduction to his brother at East Cape, asking him to give them all the help he could.

But the Captain was not well. The temperature was around ninety degrees of frost and to his great astonishment he was suffering intensely from the cold. He was having trouble with his eyes and pains in his arms. Kataktovik was suffering with his hands and feet. Their dogs, reduced to four, were worn out, and no one would sell a dog, no matter how attractive the terms. But a reindeer man let them have one of his dogs as far as East Cape, on the promise that they would send it back by some westbound traveller – a distance of three-hundred miles! He asked no payment, but accepted a razor and a pick-axe and the promise of some cartridges. Another old man exchanged his dog for Bartlett's Colt ·45.

That night both dogs dug through the igloo and fled. The old reindeer man brought his dog back to them, and when it escaped again later on the journey, he sent it back again with three travellers who were going the same way.

Thirty-seven days after leaving us at Icy Spit, the Captain and Kataktovik reached East Cape. They had covered around seven hundred miles, most of it on foot. Captain Bartlett took his letter of introduction to the brother of the Russian at Cape North. The best he could do for them was a passage on a gasolene schooner leaving for Nome at the beginning of June. It was 25 April and Bartlett was desperate to be on his way long before June. But suddenly the matter was settled for him. His legs and feet began to swell, and almost overnight he found himself a helpless victim of the same disease that we were suffering from on Wrangel.

As he lay resting at the Russian's house he was visited by a Baron Kleist, the Russian supervisor of North Eastern Siberia, who had heard about the Captain's trip and now invited Bartlett to travel with him by sledge to Emma Harbour, the Siberian port nearest to the coast of Alaska. He was leaving on 10 May. Bartlett could hardly move hand or foot. His eyes were raw and bloodshot, and he had now developed tonsilitis, but he was determined to go. Kataktovik wanted to return to Point Hope, so Bartlett fitted him out as best he could and left him to await transport later in the season.

The sledge journey through wild country to Emma Harbour took six days. Now the Captain had to find a ship to take him across the Bering Strait to Nome. He heard that Captain Pedersen, Stefansson's first choice as skipper of the *Karluk*, had been in the neighbourhood with his new ship, the *Herman*. Bartlett wrote several letters to Pedersen asking for help, and gave them to various Chukchees in the hope that one might meet up with him. The word spread among the natives all along the East Cape and on 21 May Bartlett saw the *Herman* steaming into Emma Harbour. He got on board immediately and was soon on his way to Nome, 240 miles away. But they could not get into Nome because of the ice, and made for St Michael's, where there was a wireless station belonging to the US Signal Corps.

On 28 May they were able to get ashore, but found the wireless station closed. Desperate at this new delay, Captain Bartlett contacted US Marshal Hugh J. Lee, who had been with Peary on the Greenland ice-cap in 1892 and had visited Bartlett's father's fishing station at Tarnavik in 1896. Lee had the wireless station opened, but there was a terrible period of frustration and delay when the sergeant in charge refused to send Bartlett's message to Ottawa without prepayment. Poor Bartlett had no money and Marshal Lee had to come to the rescue again.

At last the message went out, telling the world the fate of the *Karluk* and urging the authorities to authorize a rescue operation without delay. While Captain Bartlett was waiting for instructions from Ottawa con-gratulations came from his family in Newfoundland, from friends in Boston, New York, and all over the States. He was besieged by the press. A telegram from the advertising department of an American magazine asked his permission to use his picture for a tobacco advertisement.

And all he wanted was to find a ship to take him back to Wrangel Island as soon as navigation opened. The United States Revenue Cutter *Bear* was due to begin her summer Arctic patrol and was authorized to join the rescue operation. The Russian authorities sent messages to two of their ice-breakers to give all the help they could. Bartlett was especially delighted that the *Bear* would be involved, because thirty years earlier she had been on a similar mission when she rescued the only survivors of General Greely's expedition at Cape Sabine. She had been built in Scotland for the Newfoundland sealing industry and Bartlett was sure she would get through to Wrangel if any ship could.

Bartlett went to Nome at the end of June to wait while the *Bear* carried out her routine duties. It was still too early to begin any rescue attempt; the earliest time would be the latter part of July or early August. But he was anxious to get in touch with any trading or walrus-hunting schooners going north. The more ships he could persuade to head for Wrangel Island the better would be the chance of one getting through.

The *Bear* got away on 13 July. She had a number of calls to make, for besides being the mail carrier she had to bring medical help, act as a kind of travelling law court, and transport teachers and missionaries. While Captain Bartlett tried to contain his impatience and anxiety, the *Bear* called at St Lawrence Island with supplies for the schools, then crossed to Emma Town to pick up Lord William Percy, son of the Duke of Northumberland, who had been studying the ducks of Siberian and Alaskan waters. They were in Kotzebue Sound on 4 August when they learned from their wireless that war had broken out, and Lord Percy left at once to join his Army unit.

Then the *Bear* called at Point Hope where Bartlett met Kataktovik again. He had been brought from East Cape in Captain Pedersen's *Herman*, and Captain Bartlett paid him the wages due to him and gave him a complete suit of clothing which the Canadian Government was providing for each member of the party. The *Bear* headed for Point Barrow, and from Icy Cape onwards it was a constant fight to make any progress through the ice. It was anything but an open season. The *Bear* had to land mails and various supplies, and it was 23 August before she left Point Barrow and headed for Rodger's Harbour, with a fresh north-north-east wind behind them. 'The harder it blew the better I liked it,' Bartlett wrote. 'The only thing I was afraid of was that we might get thick fog and be delayed indefinitely.'

Poor Captain Bartlett! They did get fog. The *Bear* steamed slowly for days and actually got within twenty miles of Wrangel Island. Then they ran out of coal and had to go all the way back to Nome to refuel. Captain Bartlett was in a fever of frustration and despair. One gale after another held up the coaling operation, and Bartlett sought out Mr Svenson of the *King and Winge*, which was about to start for the Siberian coast. He promised that if at all possible he would call at Wrangel Island. Bartlett liked the look of the *King and Winge*: she was in right ballast for bucking the ice; she was small, short for her beam, and very quick to answer her helm. He also met a goldmine owner, Mr Jafet Lindberg, who told him he had personally chartered the *Corwin* and was sending her to Wrangel Island with a year's provisions.

Captain Bartlett felt a little less anxious as the *Bear* left Nome once again on 4 September. At daylight on the sixth she was off Cape York, and next evening she met the ice, 130 miles from Rodger's Harbour. She lay to near the edge of the ice and waited for the dawn. And at dawn, 7 September, the *King and Winge* reached Wrangel Island. It was the eighth when we met up with the *Bear*.

25   *A Pitiful Tragic Failure*

Captain Bartlett described what happened as the *King and Winge* approached the *Bear*:

I watched her as she drew nearer and nearer; then she hove to and we were soon alongside. I looked sharply at the men on her deck; her own crew was fairly large, but soon I could pick out Munro and McKinlay and Chafe, and, of course, the Eskimo family, and I knew that our quest was over. A boat was lowered from the *Bear* ... and I obtained permission from Captain Cochran to go along and was soon aboard the *King and Winge* and among the *Karluk* party.

'All of you here?' was my first question.

McKinlay was the spokesman. 'No,' he answered. 'Malloch and Mamen and Breddy died on the island.'

There was nothing to be said. I had not really expected to see the mate's party or the Mackay party, for I had long since ceased to believe that there was any reasonable chance that they would have got through to a safe place, but ... it was an especially hard and bitter blow to learn that three of the men whom I had seen arrive at Wrangel Island had thus reached safety only to die.

Captain Bartlett thanked Mr Svenson and Captain Joachim of the *King and Winge* on behalf of himself and the Canadian Government, and asked permission to transfer us to the *Bear*, where we could receive medical attention; the *King and Winge* had no doctor. This was also in the best interest of Mr Svenson, who could now resume his walrus-hunting. It took about an hour to transfer us; we were still going about in a dream, incapable of hurrying. Yet we could hardly wait to tell Captain Bartlett our story and hear his. Aboard the *Bear* with our own Captain we realized at last that our ordeal really was over. We talked and talked unceasingly with the sheer exhilaration of being alive. Yet all the time our happiness was shadowed by the memory of those we had left behind.

The *Bear* tried to get to Herald Island, but once again we were stopped by the solid ice-field. We were examined and questioned by the ship's surgeon, Dr Glanville, who was surprised to find us in reasonably good shape. Only Clam and Chafe needed hospital treatment. He was a little worried when he heard what we had eaten since our rescue, but he did his best to prevent any ill-effects by prescribing the strongest purgative in his medicine chest.

What luxuries we enjoyed! A sumptuous meal, approved by the doctor, was followed by a bed with linen sheets. But sleep would not come. I was up at 6.30 enjoying tea and toast, but the weather worsened and I had to be excused dinner. Next day I had a massive haircut and began to feel more like a human being. Then my legs and feet began to swell. The doctor tried various remedies without much effect. It looked like the old Wrangel trouble again. By the time we reached Port Clarence the swelling was so bad that I had to have my legs and feet steamed for an hour at a time to get some relief from the pain.

My throat, too, was swollen, but I managed to go up on deck at noon when a salute of twenty-one guns was fired to celebrate the centenary of the writing of 'The Star Spangled Banner'. We left for Nome in the evening and had no sooner anchored next morning than the editor of the local newspaper, *The Nome Daily Nugget*, was aboard with a host of local worthies including Scotty Allan, whose dogs had pulled us over the ice, and Mrs Darling, the Alaskan poetess. Captain Bartlett called on me to tell our story, and when I had finished, the newspapermen wanted to know more about the attempts to find the Mate's party. But I left that to Munro.

A huge crowd had assembled on the beach awaiting our arrival, but they were disappointed, and so were we. The doctor thought we would be too susceptible to infection, so we had to stay on board. Shipwrecked mariners were no novelty in Nome, but the local paper announced our arrival in banner headlines: KARLUK SURVIVORS RESCUED FROM ARCTIC ICE-CHEST' appeared alongside smaller headlines like 'Germans Still Retreating; Kaiser Offers Terms to Belgium.' Whether we liked it or not we were being treated as heroes. I could not see what had happened to us as anything but abject failure, but the easiest way out was to let the good folk of Nome have their way, and for six days, susceptible or not, we were subjected to a round of hospitality that was sometimes embarrassing. The poetess of Alaska presented me with a copy of her poems and wrote a new one praising Munro and me for our Herald Island trip.

The *Bear* received a message that the *Corwin*, on her way back from Wrangel Island had run aground on a shoal near Cape Douglas, so off we went north again to her assistance. We could not get nearer to her than half a mile, but a boat's party was sent out, and after unloading about thirty tons of cargo meant for us on Wrangel, she was refloated. As we steamed back to Nome I felt a deep gratitude to those men on the *Corwin*, the rich and generous owner, Mr Lindberg, and all the other seafaring people who were ready to go to our aid if they could get through the ice.

The *Bear* was going to take us all the way back to Victoria, but she had other business to do first, and by the time we reached Unalaska on 1 October I was feeling very ill. My neck and face were badly swollen, but there was no mystery about the cause; the doctor diagnosed an acute case of erysipelas. On 3 October I was carried unconscious to the Jesse Lee Home Hospital, and three days later I woke to find a little Aleut boy sitting cross-legged in a chair beside my bed and asking, 'Do you have Jesus in Scotland?' I reckon they had him in Unalaska too, because I was soon out of danger. 'I guess they'll have to shoot you, boy,' was how Captain Bartlett greeted me the day I came out of hospital.

I rejoined the *Bear* and on 25 October she dropped anchor at Victoria, far out from the Navy Yard at Esquimalt, where I had first set eyes on the *Karluk*, such a long, long time ago. It was only when a patrol boat stopped our launch to make sure we were not German spies that we realized there was a war on. We had heard daily wireless bulletins on the *Bear*, but it had all seemed so unreal; we felt so detached from the world. Now we had to thread our way through Japanese, Canadian and British cruisers, submarines and other war vessels.

Victoria gave us the same hero-treatment as Nome, but I was glad to be off again, this time by train to Ottawa. I said goodbye to Captain Bartlett, then travelled to Hamilton, Ontario, to see George Malloch's parents. My heart was heavy as I made my way to New York and embarked on my homeward voyage. I thought of the eager, lively bunch of us, setting out north, full of high hopes, and those we had left behind under the ice and snow and the freezing Arctic waters – Malloch, Mamen, Breddy, Mackay, Murray, Beuchat, Morris, Barker, King, Brady, and my dear friend Sandy Anderson.

The mail waiting for me at Ottawa had told me that my younger brother was under orders for service in France and I was anxious to join up with him. Perhaps active service would help to wipe out the memories of an experience which I regarded as a pitiful, tragic failure. While I waited for the medical authorities to pass me as fit, my brother was killed with the 9th Argyll and Sutherland Highlanders. It was not until September 1915 that I found a friendly doctor willing to sign my papers, and on 1 October 1915, I became an officer in the 51st Highland Division.

Not all the horrors of the Western Front, not the rubble of Arras, nor the hell of Ypres, nor all the mud of Flanders leading to Passchendale, could blot out the memories of that year in the Arctic. The loyalty, the comradeship, the esprit de corps of my fellow officers and of the men it was my privilege to command, enabled us to survive the horrors of the war, and I realized that this was what had been entirely missing up north; it was the lack of real comradeship that had left the scars, not the physical rigours and hazards of the ice pack, nor the deprivations on Wrangel Island.

There were times when I worried about whether I had measured up to the demands made upon me. But my friends in Ottawa and those still in the north set my mind at rest. They sent me a copy of Bob Bartlett's tribute to me in his book. Writing of my illness at Unalaska, he commented: 'I was glad that he was all right, for in circumstances calculated to show men in their true colour, I had formed a high opinion of his efficiency and courage. One of the younger members of the expedition, and a man of scholarly disposition – he had been a teacher – he showed no lack of grit in an emergency.'

Towards the end of the war I was convalescing from a severe wound sustained in the attack on Cambria in 1917 when I had a visit from George Wilkins, the photographer who had left the *Karluk* with Stefansson and returned ahead of him. (He later became Sir Hubert Wilkins, knighted for his aeroplane crossing from Point Barrow to Spitzbergen in 1928.) He was going to the Antarctic in 1917 in second-in-command of the Cope

Antarctic Expedition and wanted me to join them. My leg wound made it impossible, but the invitation comforted and flattered me.

The Southern Party of Stefansson's expedition returned in 1916, having completed their programme of work in a manner which won world acclaim. Stefansson did not return until the war was over in 1918. He had been given up for dead on his long ice-trip and when he told his story the geographical societies rushed to heap honours on him. When he was presented with the Hubbard Medal by the National Geographical Society, glowing tributes were paid to him by the great Peary, and by General Greely, another famous veteran of Arctic exploration. Stefansson had found three new islands; he had changed the maps of the Arctic. He was a hero.

But no mention was made of the *Karluk*. Not the slightest mention was made of the loss of eleven men, and when Stefansson's *The Friendly Arctic* came out it gave an inaccurate account of the *Karluk* affair, subtly putting blame for all the mistakes and disasters on everyone but Vilhjalmur Stefansson. It also accused Dr Anderson and members of the Southern Party of mutiny, insubordination and disobedience. And by 1921 another Stefansson expedition had been sent to Wrangel Island, where all but one of its members perished.

But that is another story. It is enough for now that at last the whole story of the *Karluk* has been told. I thank God that I have been spared to tell it. I have never ceased thanking Him for bringing me through the experience of the *Karluk* and Wrangel Island. I believe it was my faith in God that sustained me, a faith kept alive by the memory of Psalm 121: 'I to the hills will lift mine eyes, from whence doth come mine aid.'

As that great Scottish theologian, Professor William Barclay put it: 'The fact that God is on our side does not mean that we will enjoy a comfortable troublefree existence. What it does mean is, that no matter what comes to us, we can face it erect and foursquare.'

Acknowledgments

I wish to thank the following people for supplying material for this book:

Dr W. I. Smith, Dominion Archives, and his staff;

Mrs Erika S. Parmi, Librarian of Stefansson Collection, Dartmouth College, Hanover, USA;

Miss Alison Wilson, Center for Polar Archives, Washington, USA;

Mrs Rachel Grover, Thomas Fisher Rare Book Library, University of Toronto, Canada;

Miss Cuthbertson, Glasgow Public Libraries;

Miss Ann Wilson, Glasgow University Library.

For advice and helpful criticism:

Dr Alan Cooke, formerly Editor of the Polar Record, Scott Polar Research Institute, Cambridge;

Dr Gavin White, Professor of Ecclesiastical History, Glasgow University.

For invaluable work on my sixty-year-old negatives:

Mr Brian Coe, Curator, Kodak Museum.

My thanks also to Mamie and Magnus Magnusson, without whom this book might never have seen the light of day; to Miss Morven Cameron for bringing it to their notice; to many friends, too numerous to mention, for encouragement and help.

W.L.M.

List of Maps

Index

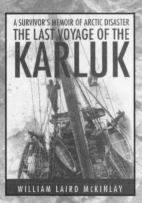